# Dairylandia

Dairylandia

# DAIRYLANDIA

## Dispatches from a State of Mind

## Steve Hannah

The University of Wisconsin Press

The University of Wisconsin Press
728 State Street, Suite 443
Madison, Wisconsin 53706-1428
uwpress.wisc.edu

Gray's Inn House, 127 Clerkenwell Road
London EC1R 5DB, United Kingdom
eurospanbookstore.com

Printed in the United States of America

This book may be available in a digital edition.

Library of Congress Cataloging-in-Publication Data

Names: Hannah, Steve (Journalist), author.
Title: Dairylandia: dispatches from a state of mind / Steve Hannah.
Description: Madison, Wisconsin: The University of Wisconsin Press, [2019]
Identifiers: LCCN 2019017146 | ISBN 9780299324506 (cloth: alk. paper)
Subjects: LCSH: Hannah, Steve (Journalist)—Travel—Wisconsin.
| Journalists—Wisconsin—Biography.
| Wisconsin—Biography—Anecdotes.
| Wisconsin—Social life and customs—Anecdotes.
Classification: LCC PN4725 .H36 2019 | DDC 070.92—dc23
LC record available at https://lccn.loc.gov/2019017146

The following chapters were originally published in the *Milwaukee Journal* and are reprinted by permission: "Of Poetry and Planting: Farmers in Springtime," "The World by the Tail with a Downhill Pull: Katie and Erhardt Schultz," "Tragedy without Reason: The Eerie Calm of John Norton," "Living with the 'Enemy': Bill Fero," "The Elephant in the Room."

*This book is dedicated to my mother,*
**RITA,**
*who, when provoked, said, "Don't get me started."*
*She's the one who got me started.*

---

*And to*
**STEPHANIE,**
*who kept me going.*

*What in the world could be less important than who I am and who my father and mother were, the mistakes I have made together with the occasional discoveries, the bad times and good times, the moments of grace. . . .*

*But I talk about my life anyway because if, on the one hand, hardly anything could be less important, on the other hand, hardly anything could be more important. My story is important not because it is mine, God knows, but because if I tell it anything like right, the chances are you will recognize that in many ways it is also yours.*

FREDERICK BUECHNER, *Telling Secrets*

# Contents

# Foreword

Lately, whenever someone asks me to write up my impressions of the Midwest in general or Wisconsin in particular, I defer or deflect. I am forever grateful to be *of* and *from* this place. I am still at home here. As a rural Wisconsin clodhopper by birth and by raising, I will always retain an appetite for curds and smelt, will always cherish any tableau that includes milk cows grazing, and will always come by my flannel shirts honestly. But it can get too easy, over time, to become so enamored with your personal perspective that you assume it is definitive.

It is in this frame of mind that I welcome Steve Hannah's new book. When Hannah moved to Wisconsin some forty years ago, he was a well-traveled New Jersey native arriving via stints in New York, Los Angeles, Dublin, and Chicago. While his four decades of residence (and close, respectful attention to character and detail) are manifested in his writing through veracity of voice, tone, and fact, it is his status as perpetual "newcomer" (forty years after my father bought his farm, the locals still referred to it as "the old Carlson place") that infuses these tales with a palpable sense of discovery, marvel, and wonder.

There is breadth of sentiment and subject in this book as well. In *Dairylandia*, Hannah's comical characterization of Wisconsin-style foreplay and description of "northwoods tavern mating" are just what you'd expect from a man who pulled long tenure as head honcho of legendary satirical newspaper *The Onion* . . . and yet when he turns his hand to the attorney who defended Jeffrey Dahmer, or tells of the eerily calm farmer who murdered his wife and children (just a short drive from the farm where I was a hay-bale-slinging teenager), the laughter fades to reveal a far more gothic Dairy State. And then—now we are back at the idea of amplifying other voices, shifting to other perspectives—in telling the story of people like the remarkably resilient refugee Joe Bee Xiong or the passionate poet Ellen Kort, Hannah does his most important writing of all, reminding us that the character of place—*Wisconsinism,* in this case—is more than what we thought it was, certainly more than we think it is, and above all forever in a state of becoming.

Forty years in, Steve Hannah is still on the road, still discovering his adopted state. It is a pleasure to ride along.

MICHAEL PERRY,

author of *Population 485* and *Roughneck Grace*

# Preface

After eleven entertaining years as CEO of *The Onion*—two of those years
during the Great Recession were not what you would call comical—I
had had enough. Geez, that sounds a little melodramatic: I wasn't planning to go out behind the barn and swallow a bedspring. I just wanted
to do something different. Why not write a book?

I called a couple of my friends who made real money writing books.
They introduced me to their A-list agents in New York. The first one, a
guy who had a fancy office in Manhattan, looked like Ichabod Crane,
only not as handsome. "So you want to write a book about *The Onion*,"
he said. No, actually, I told him, I want to write a mini-memoir, and the
*Onion* years get only a modest mention. "A lot of it takes place in Wisconsin," I said with great enthusiasm. He stared at me like a dog watching
television—that is, he tried to follow what I was saying, tilted his head to
and fro, but there wasn't a glimmer of understanding. I left after fifteen
minutes.

So I took the subway to Brooklyn and met the second literary agent.
He reminded me of Alec Baldwin giving that pep talk in *Glengarry Glen
Ross*. You know—very salesy.

"You know what I said to myself right away when I heard that the guy who ran *The Onion* wanted to write a book?" he asked. He didn't wait for me to answer. "I said to myself, 'You lucky bastard!' I mean, you *two* lucky bastards. You because with this clown Trump being president of the United States, what could be a better time to write a book about *The Onion*? And lucky me because I could sell this thing and we could make some money." When I told him that I wasn't proposing a book about *The Onion*—although, I agreed, the Trump thing made satire the flavor of the day—he was gobsmacked. .

"Don't take this the wrong way," he said, "but you're not famous. *The Onion* is famous! People want to read about *The Onion*. Nobody wants to read a book about somebody who's not famous." Undeterred, I tried to tell him what my book was going to be about—in short, about my life in Wisconsin—but it was pointless. "Come back and see me when you come to your senses," he said. The meeting lasted longer than the first one but not long enough to get through the ten-items-or-less line at Piggly Wiggly.

I called one of my book-writing buddies and reported back. He said that if he didn't need to make tuition money for his kids—mine were already out of college, so I had that going for me—he would go to a reputable university press and pitch the book. "The University of Wisconsin publishes a lot of interesting stuff," he said. "Have you talked to them?"

Not yet, I said. But then I did. And here we are.

# Dairylandia

# INTRODUCTION

## From the Garden State
## to the Garden of Eden

Like practically every page-turning event in my life, my arrival forty-three years ago in a strange and mysterious place called Wisconsin can be traced to the one overriding obsession of my misspent youth: a woman.

The Cliffs Notes version: I grew up in the leafy suburbs of New Jersey, went to Colgate University in New York, fell hopelessly in love with a woman in Los Angeles, went to Ireland for a year of drinking Guinness, ran out of money, flew back home, then tried to hitchhike cross-country to reunite with that LA lady. (When we parted company and I pledged to return and she said, "Hey, buddy, there's no anchor attached to your ass," that should have told me something. Not exactly "I'll count the days until you return.") A one-legged Viet Nam vet who drove a white Corvette a hundred miles an hour but never got a speeding ticket got me as far as Chicago, where I was instantly introduced to another woman, who would one day become my wife and the mother of my children.

So I never made it to LA.

The woman I meet in Chicago, Susan Bing, is from a state somewhere between New Jersey and California. It is called Wisconsin. More specifically, she's from Madison, which I learn is home to the University of Wisconsin and the state capital. This is news to me—and I consider myself a *Jeopardy!*-level candidate in state capitals. Of all the states I've never been to but someday hope to see, Wis-*con*-sin (the natives say Wi-*scon*-sin) barely makes my Top Fifty. I learn that this state is just north of Illinois, that Madison is maybe three hours by car northwest of Chicago, that people from Wisconsin are "Badgers" and refer to their unctuous Illinois neighbors as "Flatlanders," and there is no love lost between the two states.

Susan is pretty and funny and intelligent and, best of all, quick to laugh. She has a certain midwestern innocence—openness is a better word—and while it is a personality trait that I am unfamiliar with, I like it. She is a person wholly without pretense, and I am from the Land of Pretense, metropolitan New York.

We fall for each other. She introduces me to the family. Her father is a mathematics professor at UW–Madison, and they have a weekend place in Sauk County on the Wisconsin River. R. H. and his wife, Mary, are transplanted Texans who frequently refer to me as a "Yankee" and are justifiably suspicious yet pretty nice to me. Plus, I find this exotic corner of the earth called Wisconsin awe-inspiring. Two years later, we get married in a backyard ceremony on Lake Wisconsin. It is a breezy, sunny June day and, in the middle of exchanging vows, with the leaves on the towering cottonwoods fluttering like fingers on a grand piano, a pair of canoeists pass the shoreline and pause their paddling so as not to intrude. Back in Jersey, I think they would have screamed, "GET A ROOM!"

We move back east after the wedding. I am working my first newspaper job, as a police reporter for a daily in North Jersey. After two years at CBS News and approaching two at the newspaper, I have grown tired of the New York metro area, though it is a great place for a rookie reporter to cover murder and mayhem. We take regular trips to the Midwest. I am young and naïve, of course, but the stretch of southern Wisconsin we visit seems like the polar opposite of New Jersey. It's quiet, wide open, and breathtakingly beautiful, with the backdrop of the Baraboo bluffs shaped by glaciers that receded ten thousand years ago, plus rivers, fifteen thousand freaking lakes (more than Minnesota, incidentally), and trout streams hidden behind stands of towering pine trees along the roadside.

One evening at home in Jersey, after I cover a "janitor-in-a-drum" story—this is what the cops call it when the guys from the real *Sopranos* shoot somebody in the head, stuff the body in a fifty-five-gallon drum, cover the face and fingertips with lye, and dump it in a river—I suggest that we leave the Garden State and try the Garden of Eden. Maybe because Wisconsin is less crowded, coupled with the fact that you can actually see what you're breathing, I assume it will be more civilized. Regardless, I know it will be *different*. I point out that we have $6,000 in savings and this is the kind of big money that could sustain us for a long, long time. So we pack Sue's Ford Mustang, drive to America's Dairyland, and rent her family's cottage on the Wisconsin River for $135 a month. I figure we will stay there for a year, two at most.

As I write this, I have been in Wisconsin for forty-three years and bred two real Wisconsinites in the process. I did sixteen years as a reporter, bureau chief, metro editor, and managing editor at the *Milwaukee Journal*. And I spent the last eleven years of my formal working life as CEO of Wisconsin's greatest contribution to the health and humor of the nation and world, *The Onion*, which, as you probably don't need reminding, is "America's Finest News Source."

But far-and-away the best thing I ever got paid to do was "State of Mind," the syndicated column I wrote from 1994 to 2006. Once, as an ignorant editor, I decided to take a pass on a story—though it had an unmistakable Wisconsin *feel* about it—because it occurred just across the border in Minnesota. A guy named Sig Gissler, my boss at the *Journal* who would eventually run the Pulitzer prizes but never pull enough strings for me to win one, promptly overrode my decision. "Geography is irrelevant," he informed me. "Wisconsin is not just a state; it's a state of mind." That's where I got the title for my weekly opus, which ran in Sunday newspapers all across Wisconsin, and, daringly, even in the *St. Paul Pioneer Press*.

"State of Mind" was my weekly self-guided tour of Wisconsin—from Kenosha to Superior and literally hundreds of stops in between—during which I conducted a continuous conversation with the natives. My writing seldom touched on the actual news unless, for example, I was recommending that men in camouflage be allowed to shoot Holstein cows (official state domestic animal) after a legislator introduced a silly bill to allow the hunting of mourning doves (official state symbol of peace). Mainly I just went wherever I pleased and talked to ordinary people— many of them quite *extraordinary*, as it turned out—about their lives. Those stories about regular Joes or Janes otherwise wouldn't have appeared in print. My subjects were frequently flabbergasted that anyone might be interested in reading about them at all. More than one asked me, in- credulously, "*Do you actually get paid for doing this?*" Yes, I replied, but not well.

The most memorable of those weekly essays—bookended by per- sonal stories, the odd moment of self-reflection, and hopefully a little wisdom born of hindsight—are the beating heart of this book.

John Steinbeck, who won the Nobel Prize for Literature, traveled across the United States with his dog in the 1960s and wrote a book called *Travels with Charley: In Search of America*. He visited Wisconsin on that trip, and he fell in love with it: "I had never been to Wisconsin, but all my life I had heard about it. . . . And I must have seen pictures. . . . Why then was I unprepared for the beauty of this region, for its variety of field and hill, forest, lake? . . . . I never saw a country that changed so rapidly, and because I had not expected it everything I saw brought a delight."

He glimpsed Wisconsin for the first time in October, which, in my humble opinion, is the all-around best month of the year here. "The air was rich with butter-colored sunlight, not fuzzy but crisp and clear so that every frost-gay tree was set off, the rising hills were not compounded, but alone and separate. . . . I remembered now that I had been told Wisconsin is a lovely state, but the telling had not prepared me."

Steinbeck went home. I stuck around Wisconsin for two overriding reasons: people and place. Let's deal with this place first.

One frigid winter afternoon, I stood on the steps of the Great Wall of China surrounded by a band of baby-faced soldiers of the People's Liberation Army and had my picture taken. On an oppressively hot day inside the Taj Mahal just south of Agra, India, I paid an old woman a few rupees to let out a blood-curdling cry that crawled up the walls of that marble mausoleum and exploded at the top like a clap of thunder in a canyon. And one wickedly windy day I crouched inside a little indentation in the granite wall overlooking the Atlantic Ocean at Land's End and found myself hypnotized by the sight of seagulls sailing effortlessly on the wind.

I've also stood—too many times to count—on a picnic table high atop Owen Park off Highway 78 in Sauk County. On a clear day you can get at least a 180-degree view of the majestic Wisconsin River valley with the mist hanging like fog over the rolling hills. (Have you ever read *Out of Africa*? Isak Dinesen's stunning description of dawn on her farm in the Ngong Hills outside Nairobi, Kenya, is the most evocative piece of writing about landscape that I've ever come across. I often wonder what she could have done with the landscape looking east from Owen Park.) I've also seen the Apostle Islands of Lake Superior and Washington Island off Door County, marveled at the beauty of the Kettle Moraine from Walworth County in the south to Kewaunee County up north, made my way up and down the steep hills and deep valleys of the Driftless Area of southwestern Wisconsin, and inhaled the intoxicating scent of pine forest up in Boulder Junction.

On a cool, sunny afternoon every October, I sit on the end of my pier jutting out into Lake Wisconsin just north of the dam at Prairie du Sac. The gently curving hills on the far side of the lake are in the throes of changing color, the leaves a brilliant blend of ruby and bright maple red and glistening gold and alternating shades of autumn brown. The leaves sway and swoon in the breeze and remind me of salsa dancers I watched from my perch on a park bench in Havana a few years back.

Above me, a cottonwood drops a single leaf on the lake. The wind from the north sweeps the leaf off toward the dam where, if the spillway is open, it will tumble down into the lower Wisconsin River where the current—at least in my imagination—will take it past Sauk City, Arena, Spring Green, Boscobel, Blue River, and Wyalusing and finally deposit this single sturdy thing in the Mississippi River, about three miles south of Prairie du Chien. From there, my leaf will pass Mark Twain's hometown of Hannibal, Missouri; St. Louis; Cairo, Illinois; Memphis; Baton Rouge; New Orleans; and end up in the Gulf of Mexico. I expect it is a glorious cruise, especially the ninety-three miles from the end of my pier to the Mississippi, where whitetail deer, otter, beaver, bald eagles, egrets, osprey, loons, pelicans—yes, there are pelicans on the lower Wisconsin!—appear in abundance.

I am not a descendant of great Wisconsin naturalists like Aldo Leopold or Ben Logan or John Muir. My people come from the west of Ireland and Scotland and made their living as factory workers and coal miners in Massachusetts, New Jersey, and Pennsylvania. So I think it's fair to say that I don't come by my affection for the wild and natural beauty of Wisconsin genetically. But I have come by it nonetheless.

Even the smallest parts of my adopted state have endless opportunities to inspire. Years ago I met a retired couple from Dodgeville who had great plans for traveling—just within the confines of Wisconsin, thank you very much—but got constantly lost in the beauty of their own backyard. They took a leisurely Sunday drive through the wilds of Iowa County, past abandoned farms and fields packed with deer feeding on the remnants from the corn harvest and the final cutting of alfalfa; to hear them talk you would think they had spent the day driving through the Swiss Alps. They absolutely rhapsodized about one small, solitary county in southern Wisconsin like it was a *whole* country. Back then I thought they were sweet but eccentric; now I know they were onto something.

I'm convinced that living amid fragrant forests, mounds and bowls shaped by the last glacier, and lakes and rivers and streams that shimmer in sunlight and moonlight has been good for my mortal soul. And I am absolutely convinced that living in Wisconsin all these years has added health and happiness to my life. I've already lived longer than my father. In my family that's a milestone.

While natural beauty was the first thing that struck me about Wisconsin—and as much as it has nurtured me through the years—landscape alone would not have been enough to hold me. The people made me stay.

Wisconsinites are modest and understated. Most of my friends, neighbors, and "State of Mind" subjects abhor the thought of drawing attention to themselves. Bragging is considered poor form. They seem to have an innate understanding of humility—the rarest of qualities. Humility permits you to understand the very minor role you play in the cosmos and guides you to conduct yourself accordingly. (It took me too many years to grasp that concept.) My subjects were almost always decent and dignified and, as a friend of mine likes to say, hiding in plain sight.

I realize that those observations might seem stunningly Pollyannaish for a man of my advanced years. My late mother used to say that the people who had converted to Catholicism—unlike us natural-born Irish Catholics, who were blessed with the one true religion—were the most insufferable. They went to Mass more often, took communion without fail, and avoided meat on Fridays even after the pope changed the rules. She might be disappointed to learn that I have become a zealous convert myself, though not to some heathen (Protestant) set of beliefs—but to *Wisconsinism*.

Make no mistake about it: There are good people everywhere. (There might even be good people in Minnesota, for all I know.) I certainly knew lots of good people growing up in Montclair, New Jersey.

I remember—during a visit to see my mother, the charming and quick-witted Rita Walsh Hannah—watching a New Jersey news report about a local guy who had won $100,000 in the state lottery. They put his face on TV and, in true Jersey fashion, he used the words "huge" and "unbelievable" and "game-changing" to describe his good fortune. "Everybody in the neighborhood knows I won the money," the guy said. "People respect me. They know I've got the luck."

Not long afterward, I wrote a column about Fond du Lac's "Miracle Mile," which included a string of convenience stores on Main Street where people had won tens of millions of lottery dollars in a short space of time. One of the guys—he had won a paltry $1 million—appeared on Green Bay TV. He said it was good to win the money, he was just lucky, and the only thing he could think to buy was "one of those KitchenAid blenders." ("I like to cook," he said.) Later I interviewed a junior high teacher who won over $100 million. What I remember most about our conversation was how, when I asked him how it felt to win that much money, he replied, barely audibly: "Not too bad." I'm sure he took the family to Ponderosa that night, but he wasn't exactly talking it up.

Some of this is just the natural tendency toward understatement in Wisconsin, a place where, even when good things happen to you, you keep your mouth shut because that's the appropriate way to behave. (Plus you could lose it all if you act like a swollen toad.) I once had a neighbor of Norwegian extraction. When the sun shone on the same sort of October morning that John Steinbeck encountered, and the leaves were brilliant shades of red and gold and the sky was painted pale blue like a robin's egg in spring, I would make the moronic mistake of mentioning it. And she would instinctively look toward the cloudless sky, sigh deeply, and say, "Yes, but there are no guarantees."

I loved the line in John Irving's *Cider House Rules* where he writes about the character traits of people from Maine, the setting for the book. He says that in Maine, another place where people are loath to toot their own horn or get overly excited, "it is much more important to know something than to talk about it." I believe that same trait applies to the modest inhabitants of my adopted state.

I have an old friend who thinks Wisconsin humility is ethnic. "I'm sure someone at the University of Wisconsin has done a study of it," he tells me over dinner in Madison one night. "A lot of people in Wisconsin are Swiss, Norwegian, and Germanic. They tend to be modest. I think it's a DNA thing, and it's been spreading through the state's collective bloodstream since 1848."

I don't doubt that you could punch holes in my theories and offer plenty of examples that contradict me. I don't much care. Here's another one:

The vast majority of people I have met in Wisconsin—unlike the people I've met and worked with in, say, New York and Los Angeles— do *not* have a craving for comparative self-worth. They don't gauge their happiness or satisfaction by their neighbors or coworkers. For the most part, they don't have to have a bigger paycheck or a bigger house or a bigger car. They might like those things, but the satisfaction they derive isn't because they have something that someone else does not. They are comfortable in their own skin, comfortable with who they are and where they come from and where they want to be. But that comfort has no comparative value—at least for most of the Wisconsin people I know.

Furthermore, most Wisconsin folks don't want to be the center of attention. They are content with what they have but aren't possessed by a need to convince anyone that their state is the biggest (because it isn't) or the best (though many think it is). You can like Wisconsin if it suits you, but if you don't—or if it's just too damn cold for you in winter— well, then, go live somewhere else. And good luck to you.

I'm a great fan of the late, great author Jim Harrison, who was born and raised in the Upper Peninsula of Michigan. Many of his books are set in places that, as he describes the people and setting, remind me of Wisconsin. In one of Harrison's novels—I can't remember which one but I copied the quote years ago and stuck it to the wall above my desk—he wrote, "It was so nice to live in a place ignored by the rest of the world." The vast majority of my Wisconsinites share that sentiment.

◇

A lot of people influenced my personal and professional path, but there are two who stand out: Rita Walsh Hannah and Charles Kuralt.

Rita was my full-time mother, a part-time poet, and a devoted homebody who today would doubtless be diagnosed as agoraphobic but who was nonetheless a highly respected grammar-school librarian, her own literary tastes running to murder mystery and romance novels that were utterly unsuited for the majority of her clients in grades K–8.

She was an Olympian extractor of individual facts from people — including total strangers — and those pieces eventually added up to whole stories. She could have been a Pulitzer-winning journalist or a homicide detective or anything else that requires relentless curiosity and real empathy; she had an innate gift for guided interrogation. Instead she lived the life of a suburban housewife and mother of five who just happened to possess the instincts of Sherlock Holmes.

She was also partial to ordinary people and singularly unimpressed by celebrity. The only famous person I can ever remember her swooning over was Tom Brokaw. I met Brokaw at a small gathering of journalists at a weekend retreat in Florida. He was a very decent guy, much more South Dakota (his home) than New York. In January 1986, a year after that meeting, the space shuttle *Challenger* exploded shortly after takeoff. I had NBC on the TV in my office at the *Journal*, and Brokaw's anchoring reminded me of Walter Cronkite on the day that John F. Kennedy was assassinated. I wrote him a letter telling him how well he had done in a time of national tragedy, adding that I hoped he would accept my sincere accolades because "I don't write that many letters. My mother in New Jersey is always telling me that I should write her more often." He promptly sent me a note thanking me for my kind words, ending his letter with an admonition: "Write your mother in New Jersey — today!" (My mother promptly fell in love with Mr. Brokaw.)

Anyway, Rita preferred George from Quadrel's butcher shop, who could smoke a cigarette backward and blow smoke out his ears; Deroy Jackson, who worked for Kings supermarket and often brought his kids along to meet Mrs. Hannah when he delivered her groceries; and Ozzie

Rita Walsh Hannah, my maternal muse.

Gunthorpe, who polished our kitchen floor every Thursday night for decades, then sat and drank tea at my mother's kitchen table and talked about his family.

"Nothing is more interesting than a person's story," my mother told me approximately six thousand times, "and you don't have to travel to Timbuktu to find it."

Since I am prone to conversational diversion, I think this is a good place to thank my mother for imbuing me with the great gift of curiosity about people. "The really good things in life are learned at your mother's knee and other joints," she told me over and over, and laughed each time like it was the first. She had her people-picking priorities dead straight: she loved regular, common-as-pig-tracks people and deeply believed that there was a story worth mining—and then retelling a thousand times—in each and every one of them. She had other interests in life (ravenous reading chief among them) but none pursued as avidly as uncovering a person's life story. I observed this every day under her roof and was reminded later of something a famous American author from Mississippi, Eudora Welty, once said: "Long before I wrote stories, I listened for stories. Listening for them is something more acute than listening to them. I suppose it's an early form of participation in what goes on. Listening children know stories are there. When their elders sit and begin, children are just waiting and hoping for one to come out, like a mouse from its hole." My mother listened "for" stories and taught me to do the same.

Charles Kuralt was Rita Hannah's soul mate, though they never met. As the wandering minstrel of CBS News, he reinforced my mother's idea: in the time that I knew him, he had no appetite for "hard news," much preferring to tell the stories of ordinary people who did extraordinary things. Between the two of them, they pointed me toward the most rewarding—and entertaining—work of my life. You could say they led me to the unforgettable assortment of people who once-upon-a-time allowed me to loot their lives in my "State of Mind" and now live and breathe in this book.

And for that I am eternally grateful.

PART

# THE ACCIDENTAL AGRICULTURIST

Mona Lisa was a Badger fan. Who knew? Photo © Zane Williams.

When I left New Jersey for Wisconsin in September 1974, I took with me a smart wife, a dumb dog, a 1967 Ford Mustang, and $6,000 in reasonably hard-earned cash. I considered myself filthy rich. Had I known that one day Jeff Bezos would need to spend $28 million a day just to maintain his net worth, I might not have felt so flush. But he was only ten years old, and Amazon was a just a little stream in South America. I liked my situation.

Unsurprisingly, the money didn't last long. I had worked for a couple of news outlets out east, so when the well was running dry, I graciously offered my services to anybody who could pay. I wrote for trade publications—one that specialized in fuel oil distribution and another that served the aerosol industry—and I spent two years as Midwest editor of *Tennis* magazine. Then, after considerable begging, I got on as a freelancer with two Wisconsin newspapers, the *Capital Times* of Madison and the *Milwaukee Journal*. I was particularly keen on seeing my byline in the latter, since—according to an article I had come across in *Time* magazine—it was one of the ten best newspapers in America. For the *Journal*, I covered whatever stories of statewide significance occurred in rural Dane and Sauk Counties, such as a campaign to save the American bald eagle along the Wisconsin River and, just once, a story about a farm family in Lake Delton who got paid less for one hundred pounds of milk than what it cost to produce. Since this was America's undisputed dairyland in those days, my story made the Sunday *Milwaukee Journal* and I got paid fifty bucks.

But I needed a full-time job. Unfortunately, journalism jobs were scarce—these were the glamorous days of Woodward and Bernstein and Watergate. Nevertheless, I drove to Milwaukee one afternoon and interviewed with the *Journal*'s managing editor, Joe Shoquist. He had a big glass office overlooking a newsroom inhabited by legions of writers and editors and great photographers. He was polite but not particularly encouraging. I went home and straightaway launched a write-in campaign to get a job. The centerpiece of my strategy was to write Shoquist a letter once a month—in the third person, no less—recommending a guy named Steve Hannah for a job.

"It has come to my attention that you may have an opening on your State Desk," I wrote. "Let me take the liberty of recommending Steve Hannah. He is hardworking, pleasant, courteous, kind, cheerful, brave, clean, and reverent, and has the rest of the Boy Scout qualities to boot. I assure you, Mr. Shoquist, that you won't go wrong hiring Steve Hannah. He's the best thing since pockets on shirts."

Shoquist, a tough little bantam rooster of a guy, managed to resist my pitch for a year. Then, one December day in 1975, the *Journal*'s state editor, Paul Salsini, called me out of the blue. "We have a job for you," he said. "We need a new farm reporter to cover agriculture and rural affairs from one end of the state to the other. Shoquist and I think you're the right man for the job."

I wanted to tell him that, despite the single story I had written for the *Journal* about a dairy in the Dells, I knew nothing about farming. I couldn't tell the front end from the back end of a cow. I was a guy from suburban New Jersey. The extent of my knowledge of the dairy industry derived from two years' stocking shelves at King's supermarket during high school. I knew that milk, butter, sour cream, and cheese were supposed to be kept cold, and I had a rough idea where they were supposed to go in the cooler. I was, as my father reminded me over and over as a teenager, "an ignoramus of the first order." In short, I was a poor choice for the job.

On the other hand, I needed money, so I asked Salsini how much the job paid. He said $13,000 a year plus a new Chevrolet Impala to drive around the state. I was barely paying my bills and the old Mustang was burning oil. "That's great," I said to my soon-to-be boss. "You've got yourself a farm reporter."

Five years later I was the Madison bureau chief of the *Journal*, supervising coverage of the governor and the state legislature. Three years after that I was the metropolitan editor, in charge of news coverage in the city of Milwaukee and its suburbs. Two years after that I replaced the unreplaceable Joe Shoquist as managing editor. And eight years later, after my boss Sig Gissler left the *Journal* to eventually become head of the Pulitzer prizes, I was made executive editor. I held that job for less than a year before, when the company was on the verge of merging the *Journal* and its sister *Sentinel*, the other political party (i.e., the *Sentinel* backers) showed me the door. It was a very good run—seventeen years.

But despite all those impressive-sounding titles, the best job I had at the *Milwaukee Journal* was farm writer. I eventually learned a fair amount about agriculture and even more about the cut and character of the people who lived their lives on the farm and made their livelihood by feeding the rest of us.

But it didn't happen in a heartbeat. I had a lot of miles to cover in that Chevy and an awful lot to learn from the people.

# OF POETRY AND PLANTING

## Farmers in Springtime

Five months into my career as a farm reporter, following a particularly wicked Wisconsin winter, my boss told me to go out and find a farmer and ask him what it feels like to finally get back in the field. My editor thought this was a pretty plain vanilla assignment, but I saw it differently. Where he saw a regular hard-working guy getting a chance to cure his cabin fever, I envisioned a noble steward of the soil fulfilling his divine duty to once again make the world bloom. I had decided early in my farm-reporting tenure that I had lucked into the most romantic job imaginable. The constant belching and backfiring of perpetually gassy cows could be a symphony to the well-tuned ear. Dumping tons of hog shit in a field until your neighbors filed a lawsuit was nurturing the earth. Poetic stuff like that.

In truth, the farm beat was pretty low on the journalistic ladder, even at a newspaper in a state where agriculture was a multibillion-dollar industry. Most of my early writing made the versions of the paper serving rural Wisconsin and the Upper Peninsula of Michigan but got regularly and unceremoniously cut from the city editions, where such matters were considered remote and unimportant. So I resolved to showcase the "romance of rural life"—which I now realize sounds like a bit on *Prairie Home Companion*—in order to make my mark in the world.

Technically, my boss told me to go out and find a story about the arrival of warm weather in Wisconsin. He concocted this terribly clever assignment at the end of a long and lethal winter. Wisconsinites were desperate for sunshine. This would work out fine, I informed myself, because I was dying to deliver the coming-of-spring saga for the ages.

I drove around southern Wisconsin looking for inspiration. I ended up traveling west on Highway 60 through the heart of the great Arlington Prairie. (I knew this because the little village had a fancy sign—then and now—that read, Arlington: Pride of the Prairie.) And it was there, maybe a half mile off the road in a stubby cornfield, that I struck the journalistic mother lode: a farmer on a John Deere tractor rolling due south in my direction.

Perfect. Who better to describe the soaring state of Wisconsin's soul in springtime than a real-live farmer turning the earth?

I was wearing a white shirt and my professional reporter's necktie. I got out of the car, walked to the fence line, and waited. And waited some more. Finally the farmer and his tractor approached the fence. He was threatening to turn around when he caught sight of me waving. He killed the motor and stepped down from the cab. I realized that, since I was dressed really pretty and sported a beard and a big mess of curly hair that tumbled down to my shoulders, he was naturally suspicious. He probably thought I was selling crop insurance.

Had this man been sent from central casting, he could not have been better for what I had in mind. Middle-aged, already sunburnt, and chewing hard on the stub end of a toothpick, he wore a dirty white T-shirt, bib overalls, and a sun-bleached, red gimme cap (as in "Gimme one of them caps") that proclaimed Polled Herefords . . . The Big, Bold Breed. He seemed preoccupied. So I spoke first. And fast.

"My name is Steve Hannah. I'm a newspaper reporter for the *Milwaukee Journal*, and my editor sent me out to write a story about the changing seasons. This must be a glorious time of year for you. The sun is high, the sky is azure blue, and the sleeping earth is awakening like a slumbering bear emerging from hibernation. The birds are performing a symphony, and your old faithful farm dog is rolling in the dirt. For a man of the soil—a man like yourself—this must be a special, spiritual moment. The inexorable cycle of nature is renewing itself before your very eyes, and you are part of it. Is that the way you see it?"

I was kind of exhausted after all that blather. He squinted in my direction, struck speechless. A look of complete and utter disbelief pinched his face, and his mouth hung open. It was as if he couldn't believe that some sawed-off yahoo in city clothes had lured him down off that tractor to answer a mighty mouthful of words strung together to no apparent end.

About a week—an awkward week at that—passed. Finally, through dry and dusty lips, the farmer spoke.

"Yeah," he said, his eyes boring a hole through my head. "All that poetic stuff is pretty much the way it is out here in the field. That and the fact that we like to take the seeds out of the bag and put them in the ground because otherwise the crops don't grow so good."

Then he got back on the tractor and drove off.

I liked that straight-talking guy, so much so that I wrote this story about how he had totally—and justifiably—blown me off. It got good play in all editions of the *Journal*. People love to read about other people making jackasses of themselves.

On that lovely afternoon in May 1976, I was twenty-eight years old, probably old enough to know better. But I didn't know better. I was so carried away with the idea of being the William Wordsworth of Wisconsin that I didn't recognize how galactically idiotic I must have seemed to that farmer. But I learned a lesson—though not entirely, for I would do a similar thing a time or two afterward—that would serve me well in the years ahead: Farmers have work to do. They don't romanticize all that much. So if you want to imagine out loud that plowing fields is poetry, do it on your own time.

# THE FARM THAT LOVE BUILT

## Helen and Paul Lute

I have a good friend named Daniel Cattau who comes from a long line of Lutheran farmers in Nebraska. We went to college together. He was widely admired as one of the better natural athletes in his class, golf and basketball being his specialties. He was also a standout student as an undergraduate, then managed to earn a graduate degree from the prestigious London School of Economics in what seemed like two weeks. After that he had a successful career as a writer, editor, and consultant, and, best of all, he is the proud father of two wickedly smart and handsome children.

Dan was born in Omaha, and his arrival in the world was not without complications. His father and mother awaited a birth that shocked and disappointed: the boy was born with only one functional finger on his right hand, half a left arm that rounded off at the elbow, and half a left leg that ended at the knee.

On the day he was born—October 2, 1950, the same day a boy named Charlie Brown made his debut in the comics—there were few people who held out much hope. "Imagine the shock," he said years later, "as no one had any idea what I could do or how I could do it." Dan's grandfather Herman, a combination farmer and milkman, was not among the shocked or disappointed. When everyone else finally emptied out of the mother's hospital room—doctors, nurses, friends, relatives—Herman snuck in to see his daughter-in-law. "I have just seen Daniel in the nursery," the grandfather of seven, now eight, announced. "He has bright eyes and he'll always be my favorite." And then he walked out.

The die was cast. Dan would make his way through the world with the help and support of his family, but pity was not part of the package. He would do the best with what God had given him. He has a favorite story that illustrates his mother's approach to raising a boy: "When I was six months old, I was crawling around, hitting my head on the floor, getting up, hitting my head on the floor again. My mother's mother, a tough farm wife herself, said, '*Ach,* how can you let that little baby do that to himself?' My mother replied, 'Go ahead and pick him up. But just make sure you're around when he's thirty to pick him up again.'"

There was no more talk of coddling the boy. He was treated like everybody else. And he would learn to adapt.

At midmorning in the milking parlor on the Paul Lute farm, sunlight streams through the windows behind the four human figures working a row of dairy cows. They are silhouetted against the backdrop of steel stanchions and steam, their faces indistinguishable from a distance.

A minute passes before one of these shadowy figures—three men and a woman, as it turns out—spies a stranger in the doorway. Slowly the man puts down the hose in his hand and heads toward me. His face, suddenly in sunlight, has the rounded shape and eager eyes of someone with Down syndrome.

We have never met, but it doesn't matter. He throws one arm around my shoulders and squeezes. He is a strong man.

"Hi," he says.

I feel a gentle tugging at my sleeve. Another of the shadowy figures, this one wearing a red stocking cap and galoshes, has suddenly appeared next to me. He has a similar look about him, a childlike face all sweetness and innocence.

"Hey," he says.

"Back to work, boys, back to work," says Helen Lute, striding in our direction. The "boys," as she refers to the men on either side of me, smile and retreat to their chores. But not before I get a squeeze from one and a pat on the back from the other.

"They know no stranger," says Helen, watching them trudge back to work. "They are so trusting and friendly. Sometimes, to be honest, it scares me." She shrugs. "But that's just the way they are. Extremely loving."

And this is the farm that, to borrow a phrase, love built.

Helen and Paul Lute, who is out plowing in the field this sunny morning, have four "boys" on their farm just outside Reedsburg. Mark, thirty-eight, their eldest, graduated with honors from Purdue University. David, thirty-three, is their oldest biological son. Larry, thirty-three, was adopted twenty-two years ago. And Tom, thirty-six, a foster child, has been part of the family for more than twenty years. David, Larry, and Tom, all integral members of this award-winning farm, have Down syndrome.

"When we first moved here," Helen remembers, "one neighbor said to another: 'Why don't they get rid of those dummies and hire some normal people?' The answer, of course, is that they are our boys. That's why. Plus the plain fact that they do more than any single hired man and save us a ton of steps."

There was a time when the Lutes had to decide whether David, Tom, and Larry would spend their days in a workshop for the developmentally disabled or work on the farm. Because their boys had natural aptitude and affinity for farm work, it made the decision easy. As long as they liked it and stuck with it, they would help keep the crops coming and the milk flowing along with the other family members. They would not be warehoused during the day.

"David likes to work with machinery in the shop," says Helen. "Tom is our unofficial farm greeter, and he's physically very strong. Larry is just a natural dairyman. He's a hard worker. And he's so gentle with the cows. People say they have never seen cattle so gentle out of a free-stall barn."

At this moment, between smiles and constant waves in my direction, Larry and Tom are cleaning up after the 5:30 a.m. milking shift. At other times, they bring the cows in from the field, help put up and take down hay, feed the livestock, chase cows in and out of the parlor, and clean stalls.

"We have an animal nutritionist originally from Ireland who works with our cows," says Helen. "He loves to come out here and see the boys. And when he leaves, he never fails to stop and say, 'Mrs. Lute, they absolutely make my day.'"

Years ago, when David was small, the Lutes helped start a program for mentally challenged children at a local public school. On the first day, Helen and David were greeted by the principal, who asked that, in the future, David not enter the same door as the "normal" children. "He should go around to the back door," the principal said. Helen Lute refused the offer, but the memory of that distasteful day stuck with her for many years.

"I'm still sore about it," Helen says, gritting her teeth.

That may have been among the many reasons why the Lutes worked so hard to have their boys integrated into everyday life on the farm. And why it turns out to be such a happy, harmonious place.

Helen warns me: "Don't make me out to be a saint. What you learn from your life is what really counts. In our case, they are very special people, and we are blessed to have them with us. They are God's children. And I'm convinced that God sent these boys to us because he knew we could accept it. I'm not bragging, but Paul and I really do feel that the parents of these children are special just like these kids."

It is always awkward to conduct an interview on a farm. There seems to be so much work to do—and farmers, like much of the rest of the population save politicians, much prefer work to small talk. But on this farm, thank goodness, there are other, regular interruptions. Like all the kissing and hugging.

"If I get kissed once a day, that's rare," says Helen, pretending to be a little annoyed when Tom quits cleaning stalls, saunters over, and suddenly plants a big wet smooch on his mother's cheek. She frowns at him, but both mother and son know she treasures the affection.

"If I get kissed once, I get kissed twenty or thirty times a day by these boys," she says, feigning annoyance. "Sometimes it gets in the way of caring for the cows."

Tom, who at this moment has an arm draped around his foster mother, has heard all this before. He has an intelligent, fine-tuned tease-o-meter. It's obviously a game that mother and son have played a thousand times.

"Sometimes I think this boy would rather kiss than work," she says, looking at the stranger and avoiding Tom's admiring smile just off her shoulder. Then she turns to face him and smiles. "But he works hard and takes such great pride in what he does. So I guess I can tolerate a little kissing."

For his part, Dan Cattau, the son and grandson of people raised on farms, made his way quite nicely through the world. It helped that while his family loved him, they were determined to make him self-sufficient.

To this day, Dan makes a point of the fact that he was fortunate to be raised by people with roots in the soil. "My people—particularly my grandfather Herman and my mother, Olive—did not read inspirational books except the Bible. But they had the faith needed to say and do the right thing when others could not see beyond the immediate problem or even tragedy."

After college, Dan went back to Nebraska for a couple of years. The best thing he ever did in his life, he says, was to spend countless hours with grandfather Herman, the man who saw light in the baby's eyes when others were lost in darkness. Years later, when his grandfather was dying, Dan would visit him in the hospital. One day Herman sang a song to his grandson. It went like this:

> Out in this cold world alone
> Walking about on the street
> Asking a penny for bread
> Begging for something to eat
> Merciless, friendless and poor
> Nothing but sorrow I meet
> I am nobody's darling
> And nobody cares for me.

Dan said there were more verses to the song, all equally sad. At the end of this particular rendition, his grandfather added a question: "Do you know why I like this song?" There was a long pause while he let his grandson try to come up with the answer. Dan wasn't sure. "It's to teach parents to be kind to their children," his grandfather said.

# I'D KNOW THAT FACE ANYWHERE

## Cliff and Shelly Keepers

At *The Onion*, comedy—satire, specifically—was our stock in trade, but it was no laughing matter. The dozen or so comedy writers on staff were deadly serious about their work. Every week each writer would come to the kickoff meeting with a lengthy list of headline candidates. There were maybe twelve hundred jokes at the start of the week, and, after ruthlessly dissecting one another's work, maybe fifty made it to publication. I would sit in the writers' room a half-dozen times a year—the boss was never really welcome behind this particular curtain—and marvel at the kind of pains-taking labor that went into creating something that seemed so effortlessly smart and hilarious.

But in all my interactions with comedy writers through those years, I can't say that I found many of them to be personally entertaining or particularly funny. They were wicked smart and friendly enough but never struck me as especially fun people to share a few beers at the bar. They were, with few exceptions, uniformly subtle and introverted. It became clear to me what a huge chasm there is between the type of person who's funny professionally and the one who's spontaneously or even unintentionally funny: One might get at deeper truths, and the other might just make you spit out your beer. Occasionally they're the same person, but not often.

Though comedy certainly wasn't their job, a lot of farmers I met were naturally funny—not showy or jokey but able to wring a smile or a laugh out of just about anything. It makes sense: Humor was one of the things that got them through long, solitary days. Mind you, they weren't consciously trying to be entertaining; they were just funny in a way that was understated, matter-of-fact, quietly witty, and frequently blunt. And there was nothing farmers liked better than stringing along the coat-and-tie guy from the city.

In his massively influential and widely read *History of Art*, H. W. Janson wrote this of Leonardo da Vinci's—and the world's—most famous painting: "Clearly, the *Mona Lisa* embodies a quality of maternal tenderness which was to Leonardo the essence of womanhood."

Clifford and Shelly Keepers are standing in their barnyard outside Gilman, Wisconsin. Three pairs of eyes are trained on the side of their old red barn. We are examining the essence of womanhood.

"I think in all the time she's been up there we've had just that one complaint," says Cliff. "Ain't that right, Shel?"

Shelly pauses to think for a moment.

"Just that one," she says.

"A lady from over near Fond du Lac thought we were defacing the *Mona Lisa*," says dairy farmer Cliff, looking a little pained. "Ain't that right, Shel?"

"That's what the letter said," Shelly answers.

"But most everybody's real nice about it," says Cliff. "They come partway up the driveway, get out and take a picture, and go on their way."

"There's no hassle," says Shelly.

"No hassle at all," says her husband.

Nobody speaks. We just stand and stare at Miss Mona Lisa on the side of the barn where dozens of disinterested Holstein cows are marching toward a row of metal stanchions.

"I guess we're pretty much known for it now," says Cliff.

On this sunny afternoon in March, the object of our attention is a two-story, technicolor rendition of Leonardo da Vinci's *Mona Lisa*. The most famous example of Renaissance art portrays, in my expert opinion, a rather plain, plus-sized, matronly lady sitting sideways in a chair. Her left arm is resting on the arm of the chair, and her right arm stretches across her front and clasps her left. But it's the face of this woman that draws your attention: looking to the right of the viewer—incidentally, she looks like somebody shaved her eyebrows—she has a perplexing air of mystery about her. She looks like the last lady you'd expect to have lifted your wallet in a tavern, but, if you look closer, her expression indicates that, you know, she just might have done it. You'll never know. That's the mystery of this famous painting.

The giant canvas covers the south side of the dairy barn, north of where the herd of black-and-white cows pass back and forth, in full view of traffic on Highway 64.

It's not every day that a person gets to gaze upon Mona Lisa, particularly this gigantic, rural Wisconsin interpretation of the masterpiece. (The other version, insured for $800 million, is hanging on a wall at the Louvre in Paris, exactly 4,104 miles to the east.) This one is different in several ways, most notably because just beneath the most celebrated smile in the history of art, Mona Lisa Gherardini is wearing a Wisconsin Rose Bowl T-shirt.

The portrait, as it happens, was painted several years ago by Dennis Wiemer, an art teacher up in Ladysmith and Cliff's brother-in-law. The first take had the image of Bucky Badger flexing his muscles across the famous lady's bosom. But after Wisconsin went to the Rose Bowl for the first time in thirty-two years, Wiemer was inspired to give her a new look.

"We just leave it up to Dennis to decide what to do with her," says Cliff. "I think the most he'll ever do is change her shirt. I suppose she'll get a new shirt next time the Packers win the Super Bowl."

We stare some more in silence.

"It was all Dennis's idea," says Cliff. "He's a little goofy."

"Yes, he is," says Shelly. "He's goofy."

A lot of folks from a lot of different places come to see this rendition of the *Mona Lisa*. "Everybody's nice," says Shelly. "Last week we had a visit from a man who lives down near Stanley. Nice man. Brought us a jar of homemade mustard."

And there's another good reason why Mona Lisa is here to stay. She's not just mysterious, she's useful.

"She's pretty much the way people give directions around here," says Cliff. "You know, like, 'Take Highway 64 west of Gilman until you see Mona Lisa. Then make the second right after the painting.'"

I took a course in art history in college, and before I drove up here, I boned up on the history of the *Mona Lisa*. I learned that Leonardo probably began painting the portrait in 1503—nobody knows for sure—and the model was the wife of a Florentine silk merchant named Francesco del Giocondo. The painting is actually the property of the French Republic, and it has been hanging in the most famous museum in Paris since 1797.

And, oh yes, the "Mona" in Mona Lisa is a polite way of addressing a lady, sort of like "madam" in English.

Seeing how Cliff and Shelly Keepers have a copy of the world's most famous portrait hanging on their barn, I figure they know a lot more about it than I am able to recall from one lousy art course and a modicum of research. They must know that there was a pretty lively dispute for years about just whom the portrait depicted. Some people said it was Isabella of Aragon, others claimed it was a picture of Costanza d'Avalos, and some of the other suspects included household names such as Isabella d'Este, Caterina Sforza, and even the image of Leonardo himself.

Since I have done all this reading, I feel compelled to share my research with my new friends.

"That so?" says Cliff.

"Interesting," says Shelly.

Funny, they don't seem that interested.

There is a certain incongruity to the trudging and tooting herd of Holsteins set against the sweet, smiling face of the barn-sized *Mona Lisa*. It is one of those wonderfully incongruous Wisconsin moments where the practical and the artistic intersect.

"Has having Mona Lisa on your barn inspired an interest in art?" I inquire of the farmer and his wife.

"Nope," says Cliff.

"Nope," says Shelly.

Cliff smiles at Shelly. Shelly smiles back, knowingly. Apparently my last question was a good joke. I'm the only one here who doesn't get it.

"We like having her on the barn and all, but there's not a lot of time around here for studying art," Cliff tells me. It suddenly occurs to me—I am naturally slow, not naturally comical—that I have overstayed my welcome. "We've got just about enough to do to keep the cows milked."

Like Harry Houdini when he got sucker-punched in the gut, I was stunned to learn that—be still my heart—the Mona Lisa mural had vanished from Cliff and Shelly's barn. It's true. As near as Dennis Wiemer can remember, it was whitewashed over about ten years ago.

"At one point I suggested that I could redo the mural on the barn with that famous *American Gothic* painting, only the faces would have been Cliff and Shelly's," said Wiemer, who is now retired from teaching art at Ladysmith Elementary School. "The problem was that Mona Lisa was south-facing and the sun really took a toll on her. Then, too, I had to do the touch-ups pretty high up in the air. It got so I'd look down and wonder what in the world I was doing way up there. It never bothered me when I was younger."

Wiemer misses that old mysterious face of womanhood incarnate. He admires Leonardo, of course, but he also got a kick out of how famous his Madonna-on-the-barn became worldwide. "The picture was reprinted in newspapers—not just all over the United States," he said, "but all over the world. London, Paris, so many places I can't remember." But it's a good miss, and he was pleased to report that eventually he swapped out the Badger T-shirt for one with the iconic *G* of the Green Bay Packers. Plus he accumulated all kinds of good stories, thanks to that barn art.

"My favorite is when I was first painting it in the summer of 1988. I was up on the scaffolding, and a car pulled up to the barn. A guy got out and said, 'I've been watching you working on this for weeks. I know that painting. That's the . . .'" The guy stopped to scratch his head. "'It's right on the tip of my tongue. That's that famous one called . . .'" The guy scratched again. Dennis couldn't stand the suspense any longer. "It's the *Mona Lisa*," said the artist up in the air. "No," the guy replied, "that's not it. Just give me a minute and I'll have it."

# I'VE ALWAYS BEEN LUCKY

## The Ballad of Herman Tronrud

During my decades in publishing, I was downstream of a steady flow of "slush"— unsolicited articles, full-length manuscripts, and lots of jokes from aspiring comedy writers. Most of it was not very good, but every once in a while you struck gold.

One day in 2003, I received a package from Larry Tronrud of Hudson, just east of the Twin Cities. Inside was a book titled *I've Always Been Lucky!*, written by Larry's eighty-seven-year-old father, Herman C. Tronrud, a retired farmer from Clear Lake, Wisconsin. The book sat on my desk for weeks. One day, strictly on impulse, I picked it up. My plan was to read the opening page and then add it to the recycling.

Herman's epic—it reminded me of Dostoevsky's *Crime and Punishment*, only minus the crime and punishment—was brilliant. It was the real-life tale of a Norwegian farmer in northern Wisconsin who had the memory of a bottlenose dolphin—better than an elephant—and an extraordinary gift for detail. It was also instinctively funny, absent any indication that Herman had actually tried hard to be humorous. He just remembered the most interesting incidents of his life and wrote them down. Actually, Larry wrote them down because Herman had failing eyesight and preferred to just remember out loud. One paragraph would involve a skunk story from 1921 and the very next one a family fable from 1991. Herman paid no attention to literary structure. When something surfaced in his memory, he just went with it.

I wrote about Herman Tronrud in April 2003.

This is the season of superlatives, the time of the year when all sorts of organizations give awards for the best things that came out of the previous year, which, in most cases, are already forgotten. And should be.

In keeping with the mission of this column to be first—if not best—today I would like to announce the inaugural winner of the Steve Hannah Foundation's Best Book by a Retired Norwegian Farmer from the Community of Clear Lake, just a little south of Richardson, hard by Mud Lake in Polk County.

Ladies and gentlemen, I give you Herman C. Tronrud.

Herman's older boy, Larry, an insurance man in Hudson who doubles as his dad's pretty good part-time literary agent, sent me a copy of the book two weeks ago. It was accompanied by a nice letter saying that because I was the "author of great newspaper columns" that he had the good fortune to read regularly in the *St. Paul Pioneer Press*, I would naturally appreciate the work of another great author. Since he referred to me as an "author" and used the word "great" several times in the immediate vicinity, right then and there I knew we had a winner of this year's literary prize.

Straightaway, I called Clear Lake's answer to Mark Twain on the telephone. I began by asking why Herman decided to call his autobiography *I've Always Been Lucky!*

"Because I have been," he said. I waited a moment, but he did not elaborate. Which, now that I think about it, is completely consistent with Herman's storytelling style—heavy on the plain facts and light on embroidery.

Personally, after reading the book, I think a better title would have been *I'm Lucky to Be Alive.* It seems that almost from the moment he drew his first breath, Herman was involved in a series of incidents that, had they gone the other way, would have made his book a whole lot shorter. It started with a fat guy who sat on him.

There was an old bachelor that lived north of our place down the pasture. His house burned down during the winter of 1918 so my folks took him in. He was a real old man and when he bent over to sit down in a chair he sort of fell the rest of the way after he got about halfway down. When I was two I was standing there with my head on the chair and he came over and sat on my head.

I was screaming so loud that they all came running out of the barn to see what was wrong. That's about all I remember about that old man was the time he sat on my head.

Then there was the time Herman was hanging around the shanty near the old cabin where his dad would butcher hogs and cattle. They had been having trouble with a rat hanging around the place, so they set a big trap on the bench.

"I was just big enough so I could stick my head over the bench to see what was there," Herman wrote. "I stuck my head over the bench and a large trap snapped right onto my lip. I screamed and ran out of there. People came running out of the house to see what was wrong and they took the trap off my lip. That's what I remember most about having that big rat trap on my lip."

Meanwhile, one time Herman brought home a pair of white mice from school. They started breeding and eventually there were nests all over the house. This did not please Herman's parents, John and Julia Annette Tronrud.

"We had to try to eliminate some of them," Herman recalled, "so we'd sit by the kitchen table with a .22, and when they'd stick their heads out from behind the wood box, we'd pop them. One night my mother was asleep and a mouse crawled across her face. She got so startled she grabbed the mouse and threw it against the wall. It didn't kill the mouse but it sure gave it an attitude adjustment."

That's pretty much the kind of stuff that you get when you pay fourteen dollars for Herman's book, which thus far has been sold mostly to people with the last name Tronrud. It is long on good storytelling, mercifully short on literary gymnastics. He recounts hundreds of interesting adventures. For example:

> A family I knew very well had several small boys, and one day one of them had pushed a dry bean up his nose. After they determined that they could not extract the bean themselves, they headed for the doctor in Clear Lake. On the way, they stopped at old Frank Martin's gas station in Reeve. They told Frank about their problem. Frank said, "I can get that bean out." So he grabbed a fairly fine piece of wire, made a small hook on one end, worked it up the boy's nose until it got beside the bean, made a half turn and pulled out the bean. That's what we used to call a full-service gas station.

I like the story about how Herman and his brother Ed were driving over to pick up their cousin Arnold and go out on a date with some girls. On the way to Arnold's, they saw a skunk run into the bottom of a hollow tree and, remembering that you could get four dollars for a skunk hide, yanked him out by the tail, knocked him on the head with a short club, and hastily threw him under the back seat of their Model T Ford. They picked up their dates and, no surprise, the girls started complaining about the smell.

"When you were driving it wasn't too bad because the touring car had quite a lot of breeze going through it," Herman remembered, "but as soon as you stopped it got really strong." It put a damper on the romance that night. Eventually the skunk escaped. "I was probably glad that skunk got away because I'm sure he needed that skin more than I did."

Some of Herman's best stories took place during the three trips he made to find work out west during the Depression. He did farm work in Montana, Oregon, California, and Washington and rode freight trains with hungry souls in similar straits. He even learned how to get a night's rest on top of a moving train by wearing an extra-long belt and hooking it through the boards on the catwalk atop the boxcars, so he wouldn't fall off while asleep.

And while no one will mistake Mr. Tronrud's *I've Always Been Lucky!* for Danielle Steel's *Irresistible Forces*, there was that one night, headed home to Wisconsin after wandering up and down the West Coast, when he stayed at a rooming house in Roseville, California.

"I went in and walked up a long stairway," Herman wrote, breathlessly. "There stood a lady and I gave her money for the room. Just then out comes another young lady in a silk nightgown. She said, 'How would you like to have a little party before you go to sleep?' I told her that I'd been on the road all day and I'm tired." Early next morning Herman made a hasty exit.

"It was a whorehouse," he confessed. "What did I know? I just saw the sign that said rooms for rent." That's about as close to bodice-ripping as the young Norwegian farmer from Wisconsin gets in his book.

By and by, Herman rode the rails back to Wisconsin, married a sweet lady named Margaret, raised two boys, and ran a farm without benefit of "buying too much of that expensive equipment."

If you want to read the rest of the adventures of Mr. Herman C. Tronrud, the sage of Clear Lake, you'll have to buy the whole book.

I'm not sure it will win the Pulitzer prize for autobiography this year—I don't even know if there is such a category and I'm not going to take the time to look it up—but I do know one thing: if you read this story, written for Herman's grandchildren, you'll sure as hell—heck, I mean—wish you were one of them.

Two weeks after my story about Herman ran, I called and asked him how he was doing. Fine, he said. He didn't volunteer anything else. I asked if my story had helped him sell any books. "It didn't hurt," he said. He didn't provide much color. All I heard on the other end of the telephone was Herman's steady breathing.

"Well, there was that one thing. I went to the doctor in Clear Lake the other day. There were two white-haired ladies in the waiting room. I didn't know them. 'Are you Herman Tronrud?' one of them asked. I said, 'Yes, that's me.' Then the other one said, 'Okay, but are you Herman Tronrud the famous author? Are you that Herman Tronrud?'"

Herman thought that was pretty rich.

"I said, 'Yes, I am that Herman Tronrud. I'm the guy who wrote the book.'"

Herman passed away on August 2, 2008. He was ninety-two. His son Larry told me that the reason his father lived so long was "because of his positive attitude. It was just his nature." I'm pretty sure that had a lot to do with the fact that he had always been lucky.

# MY APOLOGIES, MR. PRESIDENT

## Wherein Our Hero Fails
## to Outsmart Jerry Ford

In February 1976, I was a very green reporter for the *Milwaukee Journal*. One of the ongoing stories I covered was the controversial campaign to build a veterinary school at the University of Wisconsin–Madison. The man at the forefront of the pro-vet-school lobby was Dr. Bernard "Barney" Easterday, an animal science professor at UW. I spent a lot of time with Barney. It helped a lot that he was patient and willing to explain things to an ignorant guy from New Jersey who knew absolutely nothing about his specialty—viral livestock diseases.

Barney Easterday and an unidentified colleague. Photo courtesy of Bernard Easterday.

One Friday night, Barney called me with what he thought was a story. A soldier at Fort Dix in New Jersey had died from influenza. When they tested to see what strain had killed him, they found it had been the particularly virulent type that had caused the 1918 influenza pandemic, which killed more than half a million people in the United States—including two of my father's siblings—and an estimated fifty million worldwide. Barney was an expert on swine flu and had just returned from an emergency meeting at the Centers for Disease Control in Atlanta. For the next month or so, the threat of swine flu repeating what had happened in 1918 was a big story in Wisconsin and the rest of the nation. Overnight I became the *Journal*'s swine flu reporter, and, largely because of Barney Easterday, our coverage was pretty good—if I do say so myself.

A month after the story broke, I got a call from the White House. President Gerald Ford had decided to invite a handful of out-of-town reporters to Washington for an on-the-record conversation. Since I was such a fount of journalistic knowledge about pork plague, I was one of the five reporters invited.

I graciously accepted. I was excited about meeting the president of the United States in the comfort of the White House—who wouldn't be?—but I also had an ulterior motive for wanting to attend: This was just a few years after Watergate and Nixon's resignation, which was how Jerry Ford got to be president in the first place. Journalism was sexy. I had it on good authority that some of the things President Ford was doing to combat a potential swine flu epidemic were a little suspect, at least according to my personal version of Deep Throat, a.k.a. Barney. And I figured it was my solemn and civic duty to confront the president and explain the error of his ways.

So off I went to Washington, where, as things turned out, I did not exactly knock the president off his chair. Instead, I got my journalistic nose bloodied. But I did learn a pretty valuable civics lesson.

My cub reporter's trip to the White House turned out to be an intimate gathering, just four or five journalists from the hinterland sitting around a small table in the Roosevelt Room. It was an impressive place, named after both Teddy and FDR, and, so we were told, it was the main place where the president conducted business when he wasn't in the Oval Office. The door opened at the appointed hour and in marched the president of the United States of America, Gerald Ford. He shook hands with each of his guests. He struck me right off as a good guy, very midwestern, humble, respectful. He made a few jokes. You could tell why this guy from Michigan had made it to the top of the American political mountain. He was eminently and instantly likable.

Unfortunately for him, I was not prepared to be quite so pleasant. I was young and full of utterly unjustified confidence. What's more, I had read in the *Washington Post* in my hotel that morning that Ford had signed a big check to buy enough swine flu vaccine to fill Lake Superior. I remembered my mentor Barney back at UW–Madison saying that he had doubts about this vaccine. So, nice guy or not—I'm referring to Gerald Ford, not me—I resolved that when my turn came to ask the president a question, I would nail him to the wall right next to the portrait of Teddy Roosevelt hanging over the fireplace. (It was the custom to switch portraits of the two Roosevelt presidents: Teddy got top billing by the Republicans and FDR by the Democrats. I read that Bill Clinton put an end to this nonsense when he was president, giving Teddy—even though he was a Republican—a permanent home above the fireplace.)

Meanwhile, I was also determined to demonstrate to the president of the United States how incredibly smart one farm writer from Wisconsin could be. He would soon learn that I wasn't some rube pleased as punch to be in the presence of a president but a hard-hitting hog writer who knew the difference between a pork chop and pickled pig's knuckle. President Ford would never know what hit him.

My turn to ask a polite question came, and, to spare you the details, instead I told President Ford everything I knew about swine flu in the form of a run-on sentence that seemed to last ten minutes but probably was more like thirty seconds. It concluded with me asking him—quite dramatically, and for the express benefit of my journalistic colleagues—how in the hell he could have been so dumb as to sign away millions of tax dollars for a vaccine that probably wouldn't stop a flea, let alone an infected hog?

I was pretty well out of breath. I was also delusional, which was a state I found myself in quite often when I was young. I was sure I had made Gerry Ford feel like Richard Nixon would have felt if he ever sat down with Woodward and Bernstein when they had the goods on him.

He waited a few seconds for me to catch my breath. "Are you done?" he asked.

"Yes, sir," I replied.

He looked me squarely in the eyes, shook his head a few times, and smiled. Then, as near as I can remember—and my memory is pretty good about these moments—he said: "Congratulations, young man. You have proved to me and everyone else at this table that you know more about pigs and influenza and vaccines than the president of the United States. That is quite an accomplishment. But what you don't seem to get is that my job is not to know everything about everything from pigs to plutonium and then dazzle you with my knowledge. Are you with me so far?"

"Yes," I said.

He continued: "Here is the way it works around here. I am the president. I get to decide all sorts of things, things I don't know that much about. So what I do is hire the smartest people I can find on a subject—like swine flu—and then I ask them what I should do. And they tell me what they think I ought to do. Then, if it makes sense to me, I usually do what they recommend. I really don't have time to stay up late at night learning about pigs and influenza—unlike you. But, then, we have different jobs, don't we?"

"Yes," I whispered. "We have different jobs."

"Is there anything else you want to ask me?" said the friendly president.

"No, Mr. President," I said, softly.

"Fine, then," he said. Then he pointed to a guy from another newspaper and invited him to ask a question.

All these years later, I remember moments like that, the way my face flushed and my temperature rose and how I wanted to be anywhere in the world other than where I was. I had tried to throw a high hard one at the head of the president of the United States and ended up hitting the backstop.

Which is how I learned my lesson: any person who gets to be president of the United States—including a guy from Michigan who they used to say played football without a helmet—is probably a lot smarter than your average hog writer.

It's one of life's irrefutable truths.

Last summer I read that Barney Easterday, who went on to become dean of the University of Wisconsin School of Veterinary Medicine, was going to be at Arcadia Books in Spring Green. Over the years he had led a lot of trips to Africa, and one of the people who had accompanied him had written a book. So Barney was there not only to support the author but to answer questions too.

I hadn't seen him in thirty-four years. We had a great conversation after the reading, and I told him the story about President Ford. He laughed hard. We promised to get together for lunch. As I was heading for the door, he suddenly called my name.

"You know, I was cleaning out my office at the university the other day, and what do you think I found? A bunch of articles written by Steve Hannah for the *Milwaukee Journal*! I got a real kick out of that. That was a long time ago." I said that I would love to see them. "Too late," he said. "They went out with the trash."

# THE WORLD BY THE TAIL
# WITH A DOWNHILL PULL

## Katie and Erhardt Schultz

On the afternoon of May 8, 1945, a hazy fog hung over southern Wisconsin. The wind was up, the temperature was a seasonable sixty-one degrees, and the sky occasionally spat. There was nothing particularly memorable about that Tuesday except for the fact that over in Berlin—Berlin, Germany, not Berlin, Wisconsin, up in Green Lake County—the Germans had signed the papers making their unconditional surrender official. World War II in Europe was over, and May 8 came to be known as V-E Day—Victory in Europe.

Katie and Erhardt Schultz at Elmwood Acres. Photo courtesy of the *Milwaukee Journal Sentinel*.

Erhardt Schultz, twenty-nine, a tall, ruggedly handsome, square-shouldered man was working his father's farm in Lake Delton. He killed the motor, stepped down off the tractor, probably cleaned up some, got in the car, and drove forty miles to Madison. Like everybody else from Los Angeles to Times Square, he wanted to be part of the V-E Day celebration. More specifically, he wanted to find Katherine Ella Knutson, the love of his life, and share that great day with her.

Katie, twenty-four and lovely, grew up on a farm near Elroy. She had been doing her part for the war effort. Along with sisters Millie and Helen, she was working at the Ray-O-Vac battery factory in Madison. When the sisters got sprung from the assembly line, they joined thousands of others in the city and headed for the Capitol Square. A few years earlier, before she moved to Madison, Katie rode a bus from home to Lake Delton to work on the Schultz seed-corn farm. That's where Katie (who was so tiny at birth that they put her in a shoebox in a woodstove to keep her warm) met Erhardt.

Just how Erhardt Schultz managed to make his way to the old Rennebohm drugstore on the Square and find Katie Knutson (she spoke only Norwegian until she went to first grade) was never exactly explained.

"I'm pretty sure there weren't any cell phones in May of 1945," said Barbara Schultz Gomes, who lives in Hawai'i. "But somehow my father found my mother in that crowd. There were thousands and thousands of people on State Street and the Square. It was a miracle."

Though people were happy about the end of the war in Europe, there was actually more a sense of relief than festivity that day. The front page of the *Wisconsin State Journal* featured a story about how churches throughout the city were packed on the night of May 8—and how all the taverns in Madison were closed. "No one," the story reported, "was arrested for drunkenness."

Five months later, on October 27, 1945, Erhardt and Katie were married. They started off farming near Hustler, Wisconsin, then worked rented land near Reedsburg, and after that a farm in Lake Delton. In 1957 they purchased the home farm from Erhardt's parents. They would live and work on that patch of earth—raising three beautiful daughters and two handsome sons—for the rest of their lives.

I first met Erhardt and Katie in the spring of 1975. The old Schultz seed farm had become a dairy farm. I was new to Wisconsin and scratching out a living as a freelance writer while trying—on an hourly basis—to land a full-time job with either the *Capital Times* or the *Milwaukee Journal*. I got an assignment from the latter to write a story about how farmers were spending around eleven dollars to produce one hundred pounds of milk for which they were paid ten dollars. Why would a person do that? I was told to find a farmer and get the answer.

A guy I knew at the Sauk City office of the National Farmers Organization (NFO to the agricultural cognoscenti) suggested I interview Erhardt Schultz of Lake Delton. He said Erhardt was knowledgeable, good-natured, and patient. Since I knew absolutely nothing about the dairy business—and I was living in the middle of America's Dairyland!—the "patient" part was particularly important. Erhardt turned out to be as advertised. I wrote the story and earned fifty bucks.

Four years later I was employed as the "accidental" agriculture reporter at the *Milwaukee Journal.* My boss, Paul Salsini, suggested that it would be good for me and the *Journal*'s urban readers if I found a farm family and spent the year with them—actually the eight months between planning, plowing, planting, and finally harvesting in fall—learning what farming was all about. I remembered Erhardt and Katie and thought they would be perfect candidates. I drove up and told them what I had in mind. I said it was going to be time-consuming and intrusive and, if they agreed, their family's day-to-day lives would be plastered all over the Sunday paper for months. Plus, there would be a photographer poking a long lens in their faces and, I said, "you can't imagine how many rolls of film these guys shoot just to get a single picture they like." I wasn't trying to talk myself out of a job; I just wanted them to know what was in store. I suggested that they might want to talk it over with their kids.

Erhardt looked at Katie: "Mom?"

"I'm fine with it," Katie said.

Then Katie looked at Erhardt.

"Dad?" she asked.

"Sure," said Erhardt. "Fine."

As for me, a thirty-one-year-old reporter still wet—or at least damp—behind the ears, it was a ticket for a great adventure. Forty years later, I would say I won the lottery.

The first article, which ran in April, set the stage.

Erhardt and Katie Schultz bought Elmwood Acres in 1957 and, once they moved their brood into the big farmhouse that spring, they were surrounded by serenity.

Looking out their back door, you see a Norman Rockwell painting of rural America. A weathered livestock barn, four huge Harvestore silos, two small boys running from barn to bicycle to cattle pen and back again, and scores of black-and-white cows sunning on a hillside.

"We love living on the farm. I think it's a shame that farmers don't always get a fair price for their product and all that, but as far as lifestyle goes, we've got the world by the tail with a downhill pull," said Katie.

The Schultzes purchased their four-hundred-acre farm from Erhardt's father. The rambling yellow farmhouse they call home was built 130 years ago and originally homesteaded by the family of Roujet Marshall, a former justice of the Wisconsin Supreme Court.

Erhardt, sixty-three, and Katie, fifty-eight, share the house today with son Steve and his wife, Terry, both twenty-three, and their two small boys, Christopher and Matthew. These three generations depend on what they refer to as an "average-size" farm for their livelihood.

The Schultz family is in the dairy cattle and cash grain business. They raise what are known in the trade as replacement heifers. "We have about 220 calves out there now," said Steve, a broad, strong, soft-spoken man who is the mirror image of his father. "They arrive at about two hundred pounds and we feed them until they weigh about eight hundred. Then we sell them before they're bred to a dairy farmer who will milk them."

The Schultzes used to milk cows, but no more. They sold their herd and have been in the replacement heifer business for a couple of years. They say it's a pretty fair financial proposition these days, although inflation tends to eat up the returns. Erhardt said they buy the calves for about $325 a head and sell them for $650 to $800 apiece. After their investment is factored in, they show about $200 a head profit on each animal. Most of the feed used to fatten the calves comes from their hundreds of acres of rich farmland.

Katie Schultz, the matriarch of Elmwood Acres, was raised on a farm near Elroy. She said the family has had to make some adjustments since exiting the milk business. They used to get a steady milk check every month. Now the paychecks are spread out between heifer sales every eight months.

"But the worst thing about getting out of the milk business is seeing 220 Holsteins out there and still having to go to the gas station to buy milk," Katie said, looking more than a little wounded. "We always had fresh milk on our table. Now we pay $1.50 for a gallon of 2 percent. At first, no matter what the price was, I was embarrassed to be seen buying milk."

"And it just doesn't taste right," said Steve, who grew up on the fresh-from-the-cow blend. "My kids don't like it either. They'll drink it, but they don't like it."

Steve Schultz values a lot of things about life at Elmwood Acres. He likes the feeling that you're your own boss, the sense of independence. He likes plowing a straight furrow and planting a straight line. He likes spreading manure and driving a tractor over a great expanse of fertile soil with the sun on his back.

"And I like having my family around," he added. "The kids know what their dad is doing and where I am most of the time. I think that's important."

People say that farming is a lifestyle, an attitude. Erhardt Schultz says farming is a business and not—although he appreciates the intangibles associated with making a living on the land—what it used to be. Was it better back then? Erhardt inserted a thumb under each strap of his bib overalls and considered the question.

"Farmers didn't worry like they do today. Maybe it was simpler. Today one person farms where there used to be ten or twelve. That's supposed to be efficiency, or so we're told. But I don't believe that one person is better off than those ten or twelve, even if he's got more land or bigger machinery or whatever. His life is really no better than it used to be."

"But it's a good life," said Katie, a gentle woman with an iron constitution and a will to match.

Erhardt nodded in agreement.

"A good life," echoed son Steve.

Over the space of eight or nine months, we spent days planting corn and alfalfa. We spent days harvesting and drying the grain to feed the livestock. We spent one day wrestling with heifers, making them hold steady so the local vet could inoculate them. To be honest, the Schultzes spent time doing all those farm chores. I mainly watched, asked questions, took notes, and got out of the way when ordered.

There was one murderous job on the farm that I was a full-fledged participant in: eating. I spent many exhausting hours downing the six- or eight-course noon meals that Katie Schultz prepared day in and day out. They were—as the kids say nowadays—*epic* meals. I got to be a little butterball, but I was comforted knowing that if something killed me it would not be malnutrition.

In one way, the people you interview and write about are kind of like your children: you're supposed to love them equally. I loved all the boys and girls in the Schultz Family Robinson, the shorthand I adopted when discussing the assignment with my editor. But, all these decades later, I am compelled to come clean: I liked Katie Schultz best of all. Maybe it was because my own mother lived a thousand miles away and I missed her. Maybe it was because Katie was smart and funny and so quick to laugh—a deep, reassuring sound. Or maybe it was the homemade bread. Or all of the above.

I wrote a story all about Katie in the summer of '79.

Katie Knutson Schultz said: "Living and working on the farm has always been the only way, as far as I'm concerned. I just wasn't designed for the city. You know when it really came through? It was during World War II when I was working in Madison at the Ray-O-Vac plant. For somebody born and raised on a farm in Juneau County, the routine of punching a clock, doing piecework on an assembly line for eight hours, and taking the same bus back and forth each day was . . . Well, it just wasn't for me."

So Katie, who celebrates her fifty-ninth birthday this week, married and returned to the farm. She's been there ever since, raising five children, milking thousands of cows, driving a tractor, planting, plowing, pitching hay, cooking three meals daily, nursing the sick, fighting cancer, and—except for that last task—loving almost every minute of it.

"I can honestly say I've never been bored in my life."

Her average workday, even now that the milking herd is gone, makes most people seem like slackers by comparison. Up at 5:30 a.m., she feeds the calves, cooks breakfast two or three times (depending on what farm chores Erhardt and Steve are doing), makes several trips to the farm supply cooperative for fertilizer and seed and delivers it to the men out in the field, concocts a six- or eight-course noon meal and also delivers it to the field, feeds the calves again, tends the books, serves as vice president of the Sauk County chapter of the National Farmers Organization, makes dinner, entertains two grandchildren, provides a shoulder for anyone and everyone to cry on, and goes to bed by 9 p.m.

The five Schultz children are scattered from Hawai'i to Colorado to Green Bay to Madison to the home farm. Raising them, she insists, was no trouble, even for a woman who worked nonstop all her waking hours.

"On the farm, when it was time to milk the cows, we just took the children out to the barn and put them to work," she said. "It seemed quite natural. There is so much for kids to do on a farm, what with work and the animals and all. I take my hat off to any woman, whether she's working outside the home or not, who can raise kids in the city. That's tough."

In a sense, Katie Schultz is the original liberated woman. State, federal, and estate tax laws to the contrary, she has always been an equal partner in the operation of Elmwood Acres. She has shared in its bountiful harvests, crop failures, and still today, its $250,000 debt.

"Behind every successful farmer," says Erhardt, who wandered in from the field looking for nourishment, "is a pushy woman and a surprised mother-in-law."

Katie Schultz, farmer, mother, confessor, amateur psychologist, is the tie that binds this farm family together. There was a time, back in 1970, when she wondered whether the string was coming unraveled.

"I had found a small lump in my breast and had gone to the doctor. He said it was nothing to worry about, but I wasn't so sure, so I went to see another doctor that same afternoon and he gave me some medicine that he was sure would dissolve the lump in a month. A month later it was still there."

In February 1970, she had surgery. The lump in her breast was cancerous. She underwent a radical mastectomy. "The operation was no big deal, really, but the treatment afterward made me very sick," Katie said. "I looked like walking death. Sometimes I thought I'd die—*other times I was scared I wouldn't.* Even when I was terribly sick to my stomach from treatment, I felt a little guilty about not pulling my weight. I know that sounds ridiculous. But I can still remember Erhardt saying, 'Well, for sure you'll never milk cows again.' I remember being out working in the barn when I could hardly navigate. Somehow, though, even when I knew I was at my worst, I knew this was not going to be the end." It wasn't. By October of that year, she was back in the dairy barn.

That episode left her with a feeling that each day since has been a bonus, and also with a distinct sense of human frailty. "I realized how totally insignificant I was in the great scheme of things. Life goes on, and even when I was so sick that summer, the cows still gave milk."

There is a movement within the ranks of American farm women—an obvious offshoot of the women's movement in general—to give farm wives their due. Not only legally, but socially as well.

Katie is not a rabid activist in any farm women's organizations. Nevertheless, she is bothered by the antiquated image of farmers as slow, dim-witted hayseeds who are at the mercy of random acts of nature. And she just hates the popular perception that farm women are rendering lard in the kitchen, waiting for the honored menfolk to return home.

She can get worked up. Farming, she insists, is a sophisticated business. To succeed, it requires business acumen, computer technology, reading an infinite number of market reports, and good financial instincts. "It irritates me to see that picture of the typical farmer and his wife—he standing in bib overalls with a pitchfork and she, with her apron on, by his side. Farmers handle much more each year than the average household. They have as much on the ball as any good businessman—certainly as much as the head of General Motors."

I think Katie Schultz has had a demanding life. But for her, it has been more than fulfilling. Has her life been tougher than, say, a suburban housewife's? "There's probably more physical labor," she replied. "But otherwise my life has been no harder. Which brings me to one other thing I'd like to say—frankly, the fact that there are a lot of farm people who complain about farming and how hard their lives are. You know what my advice to those people is? Try something else. As far as I'm concerned, it doesn't make a bit of difference if you're a butcher or a baker or a farmer. If you can't get it straight upstairs"—she points to her head—"you're not going to be happy no matter what you're doing."

One night each autumn, the Schultz family abandons work. And plays. Plays hard. I was invited—along with two hundred of their other close friends and biographers—to the annual tent party on a warm September night, with just a hint of autumn in the air.

It was 11 p.m. when the band played "Blue Hawaii." Steve and his sister Jeanne made their debut dancing the hula. The lady moved like a native, her feet gliding gracefully across the makeshift stage, her hands carving a story in space. The other half of the duo, to be charitable, didn't fall on his face once and left the stage with all limbs intact.

There were maybe two hundred people watching. They were seated beneath a big tent, pitched on the grass just behind the yellow farmhouse and within hailing distance of the Friday night procession traveling Highway 12 to Wisconsin Dells. The passing Chicago drivers, accustomed to shows with Tahitian dancers and authentic Polynesian performers imported from Kenosha, probably figured it was just another act on the fringe of the Dells' neon strip. It was not.

It was, rather, the Schultz Family's Fifth Annual Tent Party. The crowd, which had pretty well eaten and danced itself into a stupor by the time "Blue Hawaii" began, was loving it.

The music stopped and Jeanne curtsied. Brother Steve, who is better with things like cattle and corn than hula dancing, bowed and exited stage right.

A well-fed fellow, sitting in the middle of a dozen desserts, put a hand on Steve's arm as he left the stage. "Did you ever take hula lessons?" he asked the young farmer.

"No," replied Steve, suddenly puffing up with the notion that his dancing may have been better than he had figured.

"I didn't think so," the dessert man deadpanned.

It was a grand night for a tent party. The Schultz family, forever working their cattle and four hundred acres, proved they can party as hard as they plant and plow.

In Wisconsin—an inhospitable place where farmers claim they have eight months of winter and four months of rough sledding—sunshine is the most precious commodity. The process of growing food for human consumption, as well as hay and grain for the state's sizable livestock population, is compressed into a precious five-month period. It's the critical time of year not only for those who grow potatoes, sweet corn, and cabbage but for livestock farmers who must plant and harvest enough feed to sustain their livelihood until the next spring thaw, when the cycle begins anew.

Back when horsepower provided by horses was the chief means of locomotion on the farm, old-timers said the day ended when night fell and it was time to feed the beast. With the coming of tractors with headlights—as anyone who has traveled a rural road at night and seen the Cyclops crawling across a cornfield can testify—the workday was indefinitely extended.

But the Schultz family, who have only a nodding acquaintance with that American phenomenon known as the summer vacation, reserve one night for pure, unadulterated play. People come from all over and beyond—several different continents, in fact. There were two French students from Brittany, a handful of unrelated friends from Hawai'i, not to mention farmers, lawyers, bankers, and a troop of fiddlers and country-western singers who wandered in around 2:30 a.m. when the Wisconsin Opry shut its doors down the road.

The best traditions of rural America were alive and well this night—that is to say, nary a soul showed up empty-handed. There were tables piled high with salads, casseroles, homemade breads and fat doughy rolls, fruit, garden-grown vegetables, desserts elbowing desserts for a place in line. At the end of that line were big, lean beef roasts—eighteen in all. The Schultzes slaughtered a steer especially for the occasion. Nobody would go home hungry.

"Dad also had a hundred pounds of hamburger made just in case he ran out of roasts," said Barbara, nineteen, a sophomore at the University of Wisconsin–Madison. "I don't think he's going to need it."

He didn't.

If you ever spend a working day on the Schultz family farm—particularly during the planting season—you would find it difficult to imagine Erhardt and Katie forgetting the chores. They seem to be always working, the jobs never ending. Could they possibly drop all their duties and dance?

Not to worry. Katie, who gave the hostess role to her two daughters, had the time of her life—dancing, talking, more dancing, eating, chatting, going hither and yon sharing laughter with old and new friends alike.

And her husband, Erhardt, who shed his rakish railroad engineer's cap and Oshkosh B'Gosh bib overalls for a spiffy seed company cap and what looked like a Don Ho–autograph shirt, was forever in motion—dancing with Katie, then Jeanne, then Barb, then whatever unsuspecting female was left alone for a moment.

"To me, this party—and the Schultz family—represent a lot of the good things about this part of the country," observed Peter Martin, a friend of Barbara's who had flown in, just for the tent party, from Washington, DC. "In a way it reminds me of Hawai'i. The Schultzes work hard but nobody ever seems to watch the clock. They take life a day at a time."

The tent party, which had begun prematurely at 5 p.m., eventually ended. At least Katie Schultz thinks it did. Nobody knows exactly when the end came. The following day sometime.

During the evening, I asked Katie if the tent party was held to acknowledge anything in particular. She looked a little perplexed, recalled that it had started five years ago when the milk cows were sold, but couldn't define the exact reason for it. Two days later it came to her.

"Erhardt and I were trying to figure out just why we do throw that party every year," Katie explained. "Of course now we don't have any choice, really—it's reached the point where the neighbors are asking about it months before it's even planned. We decided it was for all the good things in life. Good family, good friends, good harvest, good luck, and, well, good Lord."

She meant that reverently, of course.

Erhardt Schultz died in 1992—heart disease. For the last four years of his life, he spent most of his time in a makeshift bedroom off the kitchen on the ground floor of the farmhouse at Elmwood Acres. Katie was his full-time caregiver. "My mother said it was the best four years of their lives together," said daughter Barbara. "They had always worked so hard. Now they could finally spend time together."

At the wake the night before Erhardt's funeral, the Schultz kids—all grown up and scattered by then—had displayed all the articles from the *Milwaukee Journal* series about the family. "It was such a wonderful event in our lives," said Barbara. "It meant so much to my parents. I mean, we just thought of ourselves as ordinary people living on a farm, doing our chores. But those articles gave us—I'm only speaking for myself—a different perspective. It made me think, 'Maybe we're not just some plain old boring farm family. Maybe we're a little bit special.'"

After Erhardt died, Katie stayed in the old yellow farmhouse but spent winters with her two daughters in Hawai'i. "We loved having her here," Barb said. "We wanted her to move here permanently, but she wouldn't. Her heart was in Wisconsin."

Katie outlived her husband by nineteen years. She died from complications of a recurrence of the breast cancer that first laid her low in 1970. She was diagnosed in March and died on May 20, 2011. She was ninety.

Nothing stays the same forever, which is both good and bad. It's good because change is often for the better; it's bad because sometimes you want good things to stay just the way they are. It's a childish instinct, but the child in us never really disappears. I drove by the old yellow farmhouse—the egg in the Schultz family meatloaf—in late September

2018. It is all gone. In its place, just on the runway to the Dells right off I-94, is a very large Hampton Inn. It's almost like the hotel was dropped from the sky, like Dorothy's house that landed on the wicked witch in *The Wizard of Oz*, and drove the farmhouse deep down into the earth. Of course that's just my imagination running. The house was sold after Katie died in the sunroom adjacent to the big kitchen.

Barb had suggested that I take a ride to Lake Delton and see what the old place looked like. I am, admittedly, a sappy sort of guy, but it was more than I was prepared for. Of the four hundred acres that made up the Schultz farm in 1979, about three hundred have been sold. The hundred acres left are being farmed by an old friend in partnership with the family. Richard, the eldest Schultz brother, manages the land.

It's the other three hundred acres that delivers, to borrow a phrase from Barbara, a "jolt to your sentimental side." If you stop your car in the Hampton driveway and survey the land that used to be Elmwood Acres, you see: McDonald's, Culver's, Taco Bell, Panera, Five Guys, a big billboard telling you not to miss somebody's "Legendary Buffet," Ponderosa, Uno's Pizzeria, Grand Marquis Hotel and Suites, Holiday Inn Express, Green Owl Pizza, Famous Dave's BBQ, Jimmy John's sub shop, and the Desert Star Cinema, among others. By Barb's count (she was back recently) there are at least thirty-five commercial ventures now sitting atop Schultz land. The biggest and loudest is the Kalahari hotel and conference center.

"Kalahari sits on land that used to be our woods," said Barbara. She was quiet on the other end of the line. "I prefer to remember all the good things that happened there. I choose to remember the people in our family's life, not the house and the barn and the silos. As long as we're healthy and strong, we will have our memories."

# PART

# 2

# AGELESS

*Untitled (Dancer with Cows)* by Schomer Lichtner. Screen print, n.d. Museum of Wisconsin Art. Gift of the Schomer Lichtner Trust and Kohler Foundation, Inc., 2010-065. Courtesy of the Museum of Wisconsin Art.

My first job out of school in the 1970s was at CBS News in New York City. I didn't land the job at the temple of American broadcast journalism because I was the most promising candidate. I got it because a very pretty, very calculating cousin of mine was, shall we say, "involved" with a big shot at the network. It paid off for both of us: she went on to become an on-air television personality for a CBS affiliate, and I landed my first news job at the CBS broadcast center on Fifty-Seventh Street in Manhattan.

I spent most of my time on grunt jobs for the evening news show, which was anchored by the great man himself, Walter Cronkite—a consummate professional and gentleman. In my two years at CBS News, I heard him raise his voice only once. I also worked on the Dan Rather show every other weekend. Rather was a solid journalist who would eventually replace old "iron butt"—that's what insiders called Cronkite because he was never going to willingly relinquish his chair— but Rather was never going to be "the most trusted man in America."

By far the most gracious and good-natured of the CBS journalists was Charles Kuralt. He owned the lighter side of the news, at a time when broadcast was the main conduit between what happened in the great wide world and the American people. A newspaperman from North Carolina, Kuralt had covered his share of the dark side of things but, by his own admission, had no stomach for it. He had a natural affinity for the lives of ordinary people who seemed to share that rarest of human traits: dignity. As he proved for years in his "On the Road" wanderings—and likewise as the first host of *CBS Sunday Morning*— Kuralt could find fascinating people flying kites in a cornfield in Indiana, harvesting nightcrawlers in the swamps of the Everglades, or building exquisite wooden boats in a barn outside Fond du Lac, Wisconsin.

I noticed that Kuralt's favorite subjects had another thing in common: most of them were getting on in years. They had lots of experience and lots of stories to tell. They were also long past the point of caring what other people thought of them, and so they didn't hesitate to say exactly what was on their minds. They had the unmistakable self-assurance that age bestows, and they were great on camera.

It didn't take me long to realize that I didn't want to be Steve Hannah anymore. I wanted to be Charles Kuralt. My boss called me into his office one day and said that if I kept up the good work and kept a close eye on who was sneaking up behind me, someday I could be a network news producer. But I had zero interest in that job. I wanted my exceedingly handsome face—a face attached to a head with ears like Alfred E. Neuman—to be on TV. So one day when he stopped by my desk to drop off some film from "On the Road," I asked Kuralt how I might get a job like his.

"They won't teach you anything about journalism here," he said. "Have you noticed that anybody who's anybody in the news operation has come from newspapers? You need to get out of here and find a job on a newspaper. That's where you'll learn to report and write."

So I promptly quit and got a job at a newspaper in New Jersey. The die was cast.

A few years later, I was working for a daily newspaper in the great state of Wisconsin. One day I saw a flyer announcing that Charles Kuralt was going to give a talk in Madison. I hadn't seen him in person for six or seven years, though I had followed his travels on television. I called him at CBS and asked if he wanted to have lunch after his talk at UW's Memorial Union.

"I'd be honored," he said. "I always wanted to have lunch with a guy who's got a press card in his hatband."

His talk was vintage Kuralt. He told maybe a dozen stories, some hilariously funny, others touching and poignant. When he was done, and just before we were headed for a fine dining establishment called the Brathaus on State Street, a young reporter from Wisconsin Public Radio asked if he could join us. Of course, I said.

At lunch we started off gossiping about my old colleagues at CBS. The radio reporter sat by, fidgeting. I could tell that he desperately wanted to ask Kuralt a question.

"Mr. Kuralt," he finally said, "all the stories you tell on TV involve old people." It was an accusation. "I think every story you told on stage today involved someone old. How come you don't do stories about young people?"

Kuralt laid his bratwurst down on the wax paper that passed as a plate, dabbed his lips with a paper napkin, and looked across at the kid.

"Oh, that's easy to answer," he told the young man. "I think old people are fascinating. They've been around and they know things. Plus, they're not trying to impress me or anybody else."

He took another bite out of his "fancy" Wisconsin hotdog, as he had respectfully referred to the brat.

"Young people don't know very much," he resumed. "I don't find them all that interesting. Some of them will be interesting when they're older. But not yet."

I think I naturally gravitated to older people for exactly the same reasons. I didn't need a giant of TV journalism to tell me that older people frequently made great subjects, but knowing he felt the same way certainly didn't hurt.

# TRY NOT TO BE BORING

## Emma Washa

One spring day in April of 2017, I found myself in the greatest bookstore in America. Square Books, so named because it sits on the courthouse square in Oxford, Mississippi, is a stone's throw from the bronze statue of the great William Faulkner, who sits with a fedora on his head and a pipe in his right hand, ruminating on a park bench. Lying on a table at the entrance to the store was a new release by Harold Evans called *Do I Make Myself Clear?*, a book about why good writing matters in a world where Donald Trump's tweets are considered skilled communication.

I have long admired Harold Evans. As editor of *The Sunday Times* of London, he was one of the most respected journalists on the planet. He moved to the United States in the mid-1980s and held a variety of important jobs at *Harper's, The Atlantic,* and Random House. At ninety-one, he is still hard at it.

In Evans's catechism, he offers up a brief list of tips on good writing, among them: Get moving. Be specific. Cut the fat. (Yeah, I know, I know.) Be positive. And the one that still resonates with me forty years after I got into the writing racket: don't be a bore.

That last exhortation made me think of Emma Washa. She was a feisty, mischievous, principled, and eternally entertaining person whom my neighbor Natalie Beach introduced me to in 1994. (They were, as Natalie explained it, "woodpile" relatives.) Instead of *The Times* of London, Emma's writing had appeared for decades in the weekly *Boscobel Dial* in Boscobel, Wisconsin. She was ninety-eight when I met her. I was in my midforties and had made a passable living as a writer and editor for more than twenty years. She knew that. And yet, from the moment I sat down to interview her, she regarded me as a rank amateur.

That made sense. She would write her newspaper column up until the time she died at age 105, on October 29, 2001.

I remember that we weren't far along in our first conversation when, prompted by nothing in particular, she looked me in the eyes and said: "When you write, try not be boring. There's already plenty of boring stuff out there. Nobody needs you to add to it."

Here's what I wrote about Emma Washa, who, I should add, was never boring.

The price of celebrity is intrusion.

And Emma Washa, a bona fide big shot whose name is a household word from Boscobel (pop. 3,201) clear over to Cobb (pop. 461), has paid dearly.

"Like when I was down to see my doctor at Montfort," she recalls, wincing at the memory, "I sat down in the waiting room next to a real nice gentleman. He had a broken arm, and since I had a broken arm, too, we started talking about broken arms. That makes sense to you, doesn't it?"

Yes.

"Well, anyway," she picked up, "all of a sudden the doctor appears and he sees us visiting, and he walks right over to this gentleman sitting next to me and says, real loud, 'Do you know that you are talking to a celebrity? Do you know that you are visiting with Emma Washa, the famous writer?'

"Well, whoosh, he didn't need to say that. But that kind of thing is bound to happen. You just learn to live with it."

Emma Washa's claim to fame in this stretch of southwestern Wisconsin is her writing. For more years than she can remember, she has chronicled the comings-and-goings of people in the tiny hamlet of Castle Rock (what she termed "Castle Rock Capers") and the general turn of the earth (sometimes called "Observations," other times "View from the Ridge") in a pair of publications called the *Boscobel Dial* and *Rural Register*. Everybody who's anybody and wants to remain somebody reads Emma.

That sort of grand exposure would make her a force in any major media market. But there's more: Emma, who bears more than a passing resemblance to Grandma Moses as she sits in her favorite recliner with her curly white hair and wire-rimmed glasses, will be ninety-eight on September 17. That makes her the oldest practicing newspaper columnist in the United States. Maybe the whole world.

Quite aside from having been around since before the Spanish-American War, all that concentrated viewing from the ridge has made Emma one smart cookie. For me, that is particularly nice to encounter when you are, by comparison, just getting started in the writing game and someone is willing to share with you the fundamentals of successful storytelling:

1. "Just go ahead and say it. Say it straight. Don't beat around the bush."
2. "Don't be boring."

3. And most important, "If your neighbors have gone to visit their grandchildren out-of-town, for crying out loud don't put it in the paper until they get back home! The news will keep and you don't want to be drawing a road map for a burglar."

From her white clapboard home in the hollow here, just a robin's hop from the Castle Rock Lutheran Hall where the annual mother-daughter banquet provides reams of column fodder, Emma keeps track of the news that matters. Some of it can be seen from the window of her front room. Some of it turns up when she drives over to Fennimore to run errands. (Incidentally, Emma has a one-owner, ancient Ford Maverick she would like to unload to the highest bidder over $250.) And some of the news just naturally comes your way when you have nine children, fifty-five grandchildren, and ninety-seven great-grandchildren.

"I guess you'd say our news is neighborhood talk mostly," she says, now in repose, hands clasped behind her head, looking straight at the ceiling from her reclining La-Z-Boy.

"Oh, occasionally there's a fire or a car crash. And I have a friend, Clara Hoffland, who writes for the *Fennimore Times*. She calls me and tells me something and I tell her something in return. Mainly, though, I just get a whiff of some little thing and make something out of it."

It doesn't hurt if you know the neighborhood. In Emma's case, she has been living in this locale for almost a century. She was born on a farm in Highland in 1896 and—except for a few years driving a taxi in Madison during World War II—she's been paying close attention to things around here ever since.

Personal computers and other fancified technology have not intruded on Emma's creative process. She says that she gets a lot of her ideas lying in bed, then jots them down in longhand and drops them in the mail every Saturday.

"I can write longhand as fast as any of them can type," she says. "The thing of it is, writing can be such a chore sometimes. But then, when you are done with it, and you read it in the paper, it provides a certain satisfaction. And it has definitely kept my brain percolating. I suppose it's one of the reasons I have lived this long."

She looks quite satisfied. She leans back in her brown velour recliner and transfers her hands from the back of her head to her lap. The sun is streaming through the window and a noisy tractor rolls past her home. You can just tell that, at this particular moment, the world's most experienced newspaper columnist is peacefully pleased. She wouldn't admit it, but she also likes being interviewed and holding forth.

Then, quite suddenly, a brand new thought percolates, and she speaks:

"Say, one last thing about this job of mine, which gets back to something I said to you earlier: Try and make it interesting. Sometimes people tell me things they have done and I just don't want to put them in the newspaper. The reason is that some of that stuff that happens to people just wouldn't be interesting to another living soul."

And that's when a hard-boiled, professional journalist like Emma has to get tough, right? You look squarely into a friend or neighbor's hopeful eyes and tell them that what transpired at the Annual Lutheran Ladies Bake Sale just doesn't make the cut?

"Oh no," she snaps, a faint trace of annoyance in her voice. "I would never say that to anybody. Never."

I can see the wheels turning. She's a little exasperated with me. "Don't you see how it is? I want to be everybody's friend, and I want everybody to be my friend. So I just patiently listen to them, and they see me write it down, and then I just more or less forget about it. You can do that when you're ninety-eight. People expect you to forget things."

I went back to see Emma Washa six years after our first sit-down. She had turned 104 a few months earlier and had moved out of her cottage in the little hollow to the Good Samaritan Center a few miles down the road. She was still writing a terribly popular weekly column for the *Boscobel Dial*. To my knowledge—and Google's as well—she was still the oldest weekly newspaper columnist in the world.

"A lot of people still tell me they read my articles first," she told me, as I took a seat in her room. "I suppose that's something."

I noticed her room at Good Samaritan had something like a sash hung across the doorway. Why?

"Because there's a woman here who has that Alzheimer's thing and sometimes she thinks this is *her* room," Emma told me. "She likes to come in here and monkey around with my things. I'll tell you one thing—you learn to watch her like a hawk.

"Truth is, a lot of people around here have that Alzheimer's. And you know what? Seems like an awful lot of them were teachers. I think it must be because of all that time spent minding other people's children. Jeepers, it's hard enough to keep your wits about you just taking care of your own. Anyway, I'm sort of studying it."

Emma, who never lacked for confidence, tells me that she could be a lot more famous if she wanted to be. *Good Housekeeping* magazine did a lengthy profile of her a few years ago. And she told me that recently someone from *The Tonight Show* called and asked her to come to California— all expenses paid—and just sit around and talk to some late-night host whose name she couldn't bother to remember.

"I said no, thank you very much," said Emma. "Who's got time for such nonsense?" Plus, she said, the airplane connections were lousy and "you know, it's winter! And I've got a lot of work to do." After you've been around for 104 years, she said, it takes more than a one-time shot at late-night TV to "turn your crank."

"I don't get too excited about too much," she said. "It's like this morning when they told me that you were coming to visit. One of the staff said, 'Oh, Emma, you must be very excited!'"

So you were excited that I would be stopping by? "No, not too much," she said. "I mean I was sort of happy you were coming to see me, but I can't say I was all that excited."

We spent some time talking about her writing. She still laughed at the thought of using a computer, said she has no intention of learning to type, and still persists in composing her "Observations" on a yellow pad using an ink pen. She said that when she lived at the cottage, the column was mostly a collection of social notes, but nowadays it's more of an essay on whatever strikes her fancy. Last week she opined about aprons, and next week she'll reflect on wedding anniversaries, mainly because her eighty-sixth was a few weeks away, though her husband died decades ago.

She wondered if maybe when I wrote this little story catching up with her, I might insert her address in the column. "People could go ahead and send me a card," she said. "I still like to get mail." She paused a moment and tried to gauge my reaction. "That might get me excited," she said.

We were silent for a moment. Then Emma suddenly remembered that not long ago she got busy doing one thing or another and didn't send her weekly column in on time. The *Boscobel Dial* put a little note on the front page saying that she would return next week. But a bunch of her faithful readers didn't notice the announcement, so Emma started getting phone calls and letters from admirers who were anxious.

"It was a mess," she said. "My fans—of which I've got quite a few, don't you doubt it—thought something had happened to me. I even got one call from Dixon, Illinois, the home of Ronald Reagan. If people just paid closer attention they wouldn't have had such cause for worry. Still, in a way, it was nice to be missed."

Not long ago, Emma said that one of her daughters—she had nine children with her husband, Frank, who died in 1972—wanted her to pack it in as a newspaper columnist. "I told her I won't quit," she said. "I told her it's my life. I just love to write."

Emma has watched twenty presidents of the United States come and go since she was born, so we talked a little politics. She told me that George W. Bush, whom she was not too fond of, would "never really be happy because he knows he didn't earn it." As for William Jefferson Clinton, she said he was a good president all right, "but he made a big mistake and paid for it."

It was getting late in the day. We had been talking pretty much non-stop for three hours. Emma, who would be 105 in a few months, showed no sign of tiring. As I started to gather up my things, I began to suffer pangs of separation. I had a long way to drive, but I loved her company. She was interesting and entertaining and overflowing with an uncommon supply of common sense.

I don't know what made me ask—it sounded like one of those awful, interview-ending questions that well-coiffed TV people love—but I wanted to know, strictly for future reference: What was the best thing about being 104 years old? And, while you're thinking, Emma, what's the worst thing about being really old?

She did not hesitate: "To be alive is the best thing. I like to visit with people. I love to write. I like to watch the news on TV, and especially the *Wheel* [*Wheel of Fortune*]. I can't think of a single thing bad about being 104 years old."

A moment passed. Emma gazed out the window where a round robin landed on a tree branch. At 104, Emma was an artist just hitting her stride. Then she thought of something, and the corners of her delicate lips turned down in a barely perceptible frown.

"Unless it would be that I get a check for my columns only once every six months," she said. Her voice hardened. "I'd like to be paid more often than that. Six months is a long time between paychecks when you're 104."

When I was about to leave, Emma casually mentioned that I had probably done all right writing about her every few years. She said that she figured I made pretty good money for those columns. "Well, since I'm the one giving you all that good material," she said, "don't you think it's only fair to share a little of that money with me?"

I told Emma that I had never paid for an interview. It was against my professional standards, such as they were. She was not impressed. She just stared at me. Then I put my briefcase down, pulled out my checkbook, and wrote her a check for $250. I can't say she was particularly excited.

# LOVE IS STILL LOVE, EVEN WHEN IT'S FROZEN

## Edna Koenig

A few afternoons every autumn, almost always during the cool, crisp days of October when the gentle green hills across the Wisconsin River are a riot of red and gold, I take a walk along the wooded trail that hugs the shoreline at Sauk City. It is a peaceful place to be serenaded by all manner of birds, some starting their winter trip south, singing from tall trees or hidden in the thicket of growth that lines the riverbank.

There is a laminated plaque on a pedestal at a small turn in the trail. In the center is a photograph of a tiny, smiling, white-haired woman named Edna Koenig. Above her face in boldface it says, simply, The Bird Lady.

Edna Koenig, aka the Bird Lady. Photo courtesy of Jack Berndt / Sauk Prairie Area Historical Society.

I've long ago stopped reading the text of the Bird Lady's tale. I just pause and stare at her face, smile, and go on my way. It's not because I'm not curious about why this woman has a memorial dedicated to her on the river. No, it's because I had the good fortune of meeting Edna Koenig many years ago—and then again several years after that—and I remember her story well. She is the source of a very sweet, very funny memory.

What I recall most vividly about my first trip to the Bird House was a flock of cedar waxwings flying from room to room like the Blue Angels; a pair of mourning doves perched side by side on the mantel, moving their heads in sync, watching the flyby; and roll after roll of paper towels protecting every exposed surface.

I also remember one exceedingly rotund robin that had arrived at the Koenig house years earlier—fourteen years, to be exact—for a broken leg. The break was set with a toothpick and healed. Nonetheless, the robin decided to stay. On that day back in the late 1970s, he was perched on a ledge above the kitchen door watching me eat a piece of chocolate cake and scoop of vanilla ice cream that Edna Koenig had graciously served me.

And then, before I knew it, that bird swooped down and landed on my shoulder. The cheeky little beggar wanted a handout.

"His name is Robbie," said Edna, smiling at her by-now-domesticated feathered friend. "He came here years ago. He never left."

I was trying to make a living as a freelance writer, and I had been assigned by a midwestern magazine to write a story about the Victorian house-turned-bird-hospital on a quiet street in Sauk City, Wisconsin. It was owned and operated by an elderly couple who could have stepped out of a Grant Wood portrait—Edna and her charming husband, Henry. They were utterly and totally devoted to those birds. It turned out to be a wonderful afternoon with a matched set of sweet but slightly eccentric human beings. I was happy to have made their acquaintance.

When I visited them on that summer day years earlier, the Koenigs told me how they had become the Doctors Dolittle of the bird world. They explained how they had cartons and cartons of mealworms shipped air express from Georgia each and every week, and they estimated how many trees died to provide all that bird-poop protection and how many wounded flyers had been nursed in their emergency ward through the years.

But mostly they talked about Robbie. He could follow their commands. He was affectionate. He sat in Edna's lap and took a nap. He was smarter than any bird they had ever come across. I was impressed. In fact, if Edna told me that Robbie was launching a hedge fund that fall, I would have written a check on the spot.

"He's quite a boy," Edna said with a mother's pride. "He's our boy."

It made a nice story, and, given my precarious financial circumstances at the time, I got paid well. (I think it was $250.) As an added benefit, Edna and Henry received lots of mail and more than a few donations from bird lovers who appreciated their efforts.

Years later, I came across Henry's obituary. Not long after that, when I was in the neighborhood, I decided to stop and pay my respects. The plaque announcing the Bird House was still in place. Edna answered the doorbell and invited me inside. She was out of the bird-saving business. Henry's absence was palpable. And, with all due respect to her late husband, so was Robbie's.

Edna and I talked about Henry mostly. At one point she insisted I have cake and ice cream—just like that day years earlier—and we sat down at the kitchen table. I remembered old Robbie trying to mooch a bite. I asked—gently, respectfully, the way a person asks a mother about an absent child—"Whatever became of your boy Robbie?"

"He died," replied Edna. Frankly, I was a little taken aback by the buoyant tone of her voice. I mean, Robbie had been a sort of surrogate child to the Koenigs. And now he was gone, as was Henry. Edna was all alone.

"I'm sorry to hear that," I said. "I'm sure you miss him."

"I do," replied Edna. Then, just as quickly, she asked, "Would you like to see him?"

"Of course," I answered.

I figured that, like most serious pet lovers, Edna was about to show me a snapshot of the late, lamented Robbie, maybe from his First Communion or in his graduation gown. I knew I was wrong when she headed for the freezer, pushed a few bags of lima beans and mixed vegetables aside, and withdrew what looked to be a frozen box of Hallmark greeting cards.

She walked over and placed the box ever so gently on the kitchen table next to my cake plate. The top was clear plastic but covered with a crusty layer of frost. Slowly, Edna began to scrape the ice with her fingernails. In an instant, the dignified image of old Robbie, eternally resting on a bed of artificial Easter grass, appeared.

I felt just a tad queasy. I was sure I had seen a weird scene like this in a movie. I figured this sweet little old lady was about to pull a gun and usher me down the basement stairs, where she would put one shot in the nape of my neck and then freeze me, too, simply for the pleasure of my company.

"When he died, I couldn't bear to part with him," she explained, looking at the frozen bird lying in repose. "Then, I thought, 'Why not just freeze him?' So I did. This way, you know, whenever I want to see him, all I have to do is pull him out of the freezer."

It was odd, I thought, but I had seen stranger things in my lifetime.

I stared at the box. The frost was quickly turning to little lumps of water. There was Robbie at rest, stiffer than a frozen mackerel. At the time I thought it was pretty peculiar but, a few decades removed, I have decided that it was odd but also sort of sweet. Anyway, you had to concede one thing: Old Man Robbie didn't look any the worse for wear.

"He looks good, doesn't he?" Edna asked.

For some reason, her comment immediately brought to mind my late father's wake. My dad had been a big man diminished by illness. He weighed well over 225 pounds most of his adult life; lying in his silk-lined casket, he might have been 100 pounds. I hardly recognized him.

As I stood in the greeting line next to the casket on the night before my father's funeral, a long line of people passed by to pay their respects. And what did many of them announce, not knowing what to say at that moment? The same nonsensical thing that people always say in that situation: "He looks good. He looks really good." Of course, he didn't look good at all, he looked little and long gone. Yet I completely understood why people would say such a ridiculous thing: They simply didn't know what else to say.

And so, I instantly strung together a couple of awkward sentences in Edna Koenig's kitchen that day. "He looks great," I said. "The guy looks just great." And the truth was, that dead bird did look pretty good. Cheeky Robbie hadn't aged a day. I half expected him to get up and go for my cake.

Edna looked pleased.

When I heard awhile later that Edna had died—strange as it seems—I wondered what in the world had become of the robin in a box? Years later I was told that in the diary she kept religiously, she had asked that Robbie be buried with her, but I was not able to nail that down. Like a lot of other mysteries in my life, I guess I'll never know. But it wouldn't have surprised me one bit.

When I first wrote that magazine story about the Bird House, I did what any dutiful son would do: I sent a copy to my mother in New Jersey, who was worried about how her prodigal son was making a living in a place that didn't have decent—in her considered opinion—cable TV. That was a mistake. My mother, who spent most of her life inhaling cartons of Pall Mall cigarettes while reading detective novels and poetry, had a very peculiar sense of what was and what was not "normal," one of her favorite words. It didn't matter that she herself was nobody's version of normal; in her own mind, she was the universal but unrecognized arbiter of "normal."

She read the story and called me. "Very nice," she said from her perch a thousand miles east in the pantry off the old kitchen. "But I'll tell you one thing—those people are not normal. Especially that old woman who thinks the robin is her child. It's a bird, not a kid. I'm telling you that woman is not normal."

Personally, I like to think that I was older and more tolerant, but I want to say here and now that I never kept or thought about keeping a deceased pet—robin, dog, cat, or goldfish—in the freezer. But if that sweet old Bird Lady derived some degree of comfort from keeping a robin on ice, that's fine by me, normal or not. She loved birds, and she wasn't hurting another living soul. Quite the contrary, she devoted her life to helping all small creatures with a beating heart. Plus, who can really explain this thing called love?

# BEAUTIFUL BALLERINAS, HEAVENLY HOLSTEINS

## The Life and Loves of Schomer Lichtner

The art that graces the walls of my home traces the path of my life.

There is a framed print of two ladies and a straw-hatted gentleman tiptoeing through wet sand at low tide on the Mediterranean coast of Italy. I found it at a studio in Florence where my son, Brendan, spent a semester in college mastering the mysteries of the Sangiovese grape when he should have been learning to speak enough Italian to graduate.

On another wall is a collection of delicate paper cuttings, some framed in red bamboo, purchased in a back-alley art studio in Shanghai. They depict brightly colored birds perched on twisted tree branches at the edge

Schomer Lichtner, a boyish old master. Photo courtesy of R. Smith.

of a cliff. They share a wall with a painting of a seductive Indian beauty astride a bejeweled elephant. That one is called *The Wedding Procession*, and I bought it in Ahmedabad, India, on the banks of the Sabarmati River, on a round-the-world reporting trip thirty-eight years ago.

On a bedroom wall is a stunning photograph, long and deep, of an endless expanse of golden desert with a solitary tree defiantly rooted in sand. It is the only sign of life in the scene. It was given to me in 2005 by my old friend Brady Williamson, who got it from a *National Geographic* photographer during a trip to South Sudan, where Brady worked on a new constitution for the Sudanese. I admired it, and he arranged to have it hung on my office wall one day when I was out of town.

There are dozens of other pieces, including a painting I bought in 2015 from a young artist in Havana, three bold molas given to me by a doctor friend who left Madison for Panama and spent a year walking barefoot from village to village inoculating children, and a farm field below the mountaintop town of Casole d'Elsa in Tuscany bordered by a row of cypress trees that remind me of that dream sequence in the movie *Gladiator*. My art collection will never be auctioned at Sotheby's, but there's a deeply personal story behind every piece.

My hands-down favorite is a colorful print titled *Wisconsin Landscape* by my favorite Wisconsin artist, Schomer Lichtner. It is an abstract interpretation of a lush, green, pyramid-shaped hill featuring a herd of black-and-white cows, a brilliant sun shining overhead. A little patch of corn at the bottom-right corner bears Schomer's whimsical trademark—a ballerina no bigger than Tinker Bell gliding gracefully over cornstalks.

Schomer Lichtner was ninety-three years young when we met. His is the undisputed happiest piece of art I own, and it occupies a strategic spot in my home because I want to see it first thing every morning. Schomer was a happy person and a happy painter—there was no trace of the brooding artiste in him. He gave me that print unexpectedly in 1997 after he had already given me another gift: the story of his long and productive life.

I am sitting in Schomer Lichtner's studio, surrounded by dozens of paintings of rolling midwestern hills dotted by herds of lolling black-and-white cows standing directly in the path of delicate ballerinas falling to earth with parasols slowing their descent. He is an accomplished and astonishingly prolific artist. I have admired his work for years, but this is the first time I have met him. My friend Bob Smith is a relative of the artist's, twice removed by marriage. He takes me to Schomer's home and makes the introduction. After two hours of showing me his work and talking about a career that has spanned more than seven decades, he has a confession to make.

"A few years ago I never would have been able to sit down like this and speak with you," he says. His wife, Ruth Grotenrath, died ten years earlier. She was also an accomplished artist, more commercially successful than her husband. And she was something else in their marriage: the outgoing one, the person to whom talking with strangers came naturally, the conversationally adept half of their fifty-four-year marriage who negotiated virtually all of the couple's social commerce.

"I was always too shy," says Schomer. "I didn't really think people liked me. But I am ninety-three and past that now. I have finally learned to accept myself, my work, my ideas. I think Ruth would be proud of me."

This is quickly turning into some kind of confessional. He tells me that he has another secret to divulge: he loves women, particularly ballerinas and belly dancers.

"I am fascinated by ballerinas," he says. "The poses are so marvelously beautiful. The lines are so graceful. I would have to say that the most beautiful nude model I have ever drawn was nowhere near as captivating as a ballerina fully clothed."

A shocking admission from a man your age, Schomer.

"No," the artist says. "Shocking is when my friends decided to throw a party for my ninetieth birthday. They arranged for a belly dancer to come and entertain. She was wonderful! And when she heard that I liked painting cows, she announced that she worked with cows too."

Really? Schomer said.

"Yes," she told him. "When I'm not belly dancing, I'm a veterinarian."

Schomer Lichtner worked in his father's coffee business when he was a young boy. His job was to pack premiums in boxes. One day he came across an Oriental print stuck in a box with a dish. He was transfixed by the beauty and mystery of the pattern and colors.

"It was just a picture in a premium box," he says, "but it was enough." He demonstrated aptitude in art and was invited to join a painting class. His mother thought it would be nice if young Schomer also studied piano.

"I never practiced," he recalls. "One day my teacher said, 'Don't you ever want to make something of yourself?' And I said, 'Yes, I want to make myself an artist.'"

From then on it was nothing but art. Schomer studied art at the University of Wisconsin and took courses at the Art Students League in

New York and the Art Institute of Chicago. In 1934 he married Ruth. It was the perfect partnership of love and art that lasted until her death in 1988.

"We worked together," says Schomer, whose studio is full of Ruth's paintings—bright, colorful, uplifting scenes drawn from everyday surroundings. "For a while we worked in the same studio, but there was a problem. She would look at what I was doing and say, 'Oh, that's good.' It was fatal. I was tempted to stop immediately. So we built a dividing wall in the studio and then we imposed the 'no comment' rule. It meant we did not comment on each other's work unless asked."

In the 1930s, Schomer and Ruth got commissions from the artistic end of the federal government's Works Progress Administration, a program designed to put starving artists to work during the Great Depression. They set about doing murals for schools and other public spaces. Ruth did a mural for the post office up in Hudson, Wisconsin, while Schomer painted landscapes elsewhere in Wisconsin, Kentucky, and Michigan. They were paid ninety-eight cents an hour. And they were happy for it.

As part of the WPA program, Schomer also painted a picture of farmworkers harvesting potatoes in a field near Wisconsin Rapids, a long-stored image he retained in his memory from one summer working on a farm. It was called, cleverly enough, *The Potato Pickers*, and it was so striking that President Franklin D. Roosevelt had it hung in the White House.

"That was nice," says Schomer, a man given to understatement. "I have no idea what became of it."

When they were first married, Schomer and Ruth lived and painted in a cabin in a pasture near Holy Hill in Washington County. There were cows everywhere. One day a brassy old bossy stuck her head in the window of the cabin to see what the artists were up to. Schomer liked that. It inspired him.

"I always liked cows," he says. "They seem to be just about everywhere in Wisconsin. You had to watch where you stepped."

His attachment to ballet began in his late fifties. Since then, he has done hundreds of paintings and wooden sculptures that, improbably but beautifully, marry bovines and ballet. The ballerinas in Schomer's paintings are often parachuting by parasol to the pasture below or delicately landing on or dancing across the bony backs of black-and-whites.

There isn't any great method or mystery to it, Schomer says. "I just put ballerinas and cows in my paintings whenever and wherever I could."

It is a fine thing, says Schomer, to be ninety-three and healthy and full of flights of fancy that find their way onto canvas. It wasn't always so. When Ruth died, Schomer found himself personally and professionally adrift. He is shy by nature and, practically overnight, had to learn to deal with people. So with the help of his friends and admirers—and also, no doubt, thanks to the natural, magnetic kindness he exudes—he learned to deal with his fellow human beings.

Now, a decade out on his own, Schomer Lichtner has reached the point where he is no longer *afraid* of people. Nor does he need their approval, as he once did. "It's true," he says. "I don't really *need* anyone's approval."

He looks seriously satisfied for a second or two. Then he smiles from ear to ear and winks in my direction.

"But I don't really *mind* it either," he says.

I think of Schomer Lichtner a lot, prompted by several prints and pen-and-ink sketches that hang in my home and a colorful coffee-table book given to me by my children, Brendan and Jamie, that rests on a table in front of the fireplace. Together they tell the story of an uncharacteristically contented artist who spent eight decades doing exactly what he wanted with his life.

Schomer was 101 when he passed away at his home on the East Side of Milwaukee, surrounded by a company of elegant ballerinas and a herd of happy cows.

He was a shy and diffident man who eventually learned to let people get to know him. It surprised him just how much he liked that feeling. And if you happened to be one of those people he let into his orbit—even for a brief time, as I was—your life was infinitely richer for it.

# LARGER THAN LIFE, SUDDENLY SMALL

## Eric Lloyd Wright

I can still switch on the old black-and-white TV that sits in the corner of my memory and watch a young Mike Wallace, shrouded in a fog of cigarette smoke, interview Frank Lloyd Wright in 1957. Wright was ninety years old and overseeing construction of the Guggenheim Museum in New York. While Wallace waves his cigarette and shuffles his notes, Wright leans back in calm repose, looking almost bored, like a model who has posed a little too long for a sculptor.

At one point, Wallace says that Wright had been quoted saying that if he had fifteen more years on planet Earth, "he could rebuild this entire country." And Wright, casually scratching his eyelid, looking mildly amused, replies, "I did say that and it's true." He says that he's designed 769 buildings worldwide, and, even in the late innings of his career, he can "shake them [new buildings] out of his sleeve." That's how easy it is for a genius to generate ideas.

"If I said I was the greatest architect in the world," adds Wright, "I don't think it would be very arrogant."

I'm not qualified to select the greatest architect in the world. But I'd probably say that Frank Lloyd Wright is the most famous person to ever come out of Wisconsin.

My cottage on the Wisconsin River is about twenty miles from Taliesin, Wright's home and studio that sits on a brow overlooking a stretch of Highway 23 on the west side of Spring Green. I have toured this monument to prairie style architecture a number of times, along with Taliesin West in Scottsdale, Arizona. I've been to the Seth Peterson cottage near Mirror Lake and seen lots of Wright-designed homes in Oak Park, outside Chicago. I've read several biographies of Wright, and there's a massive book of photographs of his buildings that has claimed a big chunk of the coffee table at my home on the river.

I'm sure the proximity of my place to Taliesin accounts, in part, for my fascination with Frank Lloyd Wright. However, my interest mainly stems from his larger-than-life character. He was a genius, a rebel, a rake, a thorn in the side of the establishment, a constant source of gossip and scandal, a person who always lived beyond his means, and—despite the fact he is still something of a cottage industry in Spring Green—a man remembered as a deadbeat who didn't pay his bills. I haven't even touched on lots of other accolades and controversies involving Wright. I don't think anyone can dispute that the verifiable events of his life—some of the "facts," including a number in his autobiography, seem questionable—are far more interesting than most fiction.

I never met Frank Lloyd Wright, which figures because I was a kid trying out for Little League baseball in New Jersey when he died in April 1959. But four decades later, in March 1999, I had a memorable dinner with his grandson, Eric Lloyd Wright, at the Lake Park Bistro in Milwaukee.

From his distinctive cheekbones to the shape of his face and particularly the light in his eyes, the man sitting across the dinner table looks remarkably like Frank Lloyd Wright. He comes by the resemblance honestly. His name is Eric Lloyd Wright, and besides being a successful architect in his own right, he is the great man's grandson and keeper of the family architectural flame.

Being the grandson of Mr. Wright—he refers to him, with warmth and affection, as "grandfather"—has been both a blessing and a burden.

The blessing? "I worked alongside my grandfather at Taliesin for eight years, from 1948 to 1956, and it was wonderful," says Eric, whose own father, also an accomplished architect, was Frank Lloyd Wright Jr. "Anyone who had the opportunity to learn from my grandfather at Taliesin will tell you that it was one of the most important experiences of their life. We were very lucky."

And the burden? "He was very tough on those who were closest to him, and I was very close to him," he says. "Then, too, there is a great responsibility that comes with carrying on my grandfather's work, carrying on the name. It demands quite a bit of time away from your own work."

There is something of a Frank Lloyd Wright revival afoot these days. (There always is.) It's hard to pick up a magazine without encountering some reference to Wright's legacy, whether it's an essay in *Time* on his place in architectural history or a feature in *Vanity Fair* recounting famous clashes with clients—he was always over budget and unapologetic—or the scandalous details of his unconventional love life.

Just last year, Ken Burns, the brilliant filmmaker who has given us everything from the histories of baseball and jazz to Lewis and Clark's expedition, directed a fascinating documentary for PBS on the life of Frank Lloyd Wright. There's a touching scene at the end, when Eric tearfully recalls the day his grandfather died. Eric Lloyd Wright looked maybe 50 in the film. It didn't seem to add up.

"That's because I'm actually 69," he tells me. "My grandfather was 91 when he died. My father was 88. And I just recently lost my uncle Dave. He was 103. The Wrights have pretty good genes."

We cover the conversational waterfront over dinner: the financial problems that have plagued Wright's home and studio, Taliesin; his rich memories of time spent studying under his grandfather; how terribly upset family members were when Frank Lloyd Wright's remains were exhumed from his Wisconsin plot and moved to Arizona, as directed by his widow, Olgivanna; his own architectural career, designing private residences and office buildings and churches from his studio in Malibu, California; and the home overlooking the Pacific Ocean that he has been building for the past eight years.

But mostly the grandson talks about what he calls the "love-hate relationship between my grandfather and Wisconsin."

"People were shocked by many of the things my grandfather did back then," he says, "things that would shock absolutely no one today." Things, Eric says, like running off to Europe with the wife of a client; living out of wedlock long before it became fashionable; and, something you can still hear in Spring Green today, the cavalier way in which Frank Lloyd Wright regarded money. And debt.

"My grandfather used to say, 'Take care of the luxuries in life and the necessities will take care of themselves,'" Eric remembers. It was not a philosophy that sat well with a lot of local people, particularly people to whom his grandfather owed money for their work.

Now and then, Eric Lloyd Wright laughs a little when he recounts some of his grandfather's deeds. It is a laugh that seems more nervous than humorous. It's obvious that even after all these years—four decades since Frank Lloyd Wright, born in Richland Center in 1867, passed on—he would really like the people of Wisconsin to revere the memory of his grandfather.

"Or at least try to understand him."

He says his grandfather was independent and unconventional and was a hometown prophet who—while worshipped the world over—was not honored in his own home state, at least not during his lifetime. It was the arrogance and flamboyance and flouting of convention that didn't sit well with the inherent modesty of Wisconsin people. His grandfather, he says, remains misunderstood.

The idea that Frank Lloyd Wright went around building monuments to himself—which you still hear people say—is stupid, says the grandson. "My grandfather's dream was to build a beautiful environment for everyone," says Eric. "He was particularly interested in improving the lot of the ordinary citizen."

Eric Lloyd Wright says that what Frank Lloyd Wright wanted—and this is what so many people in Wisconsin and elsewhere never quite grasped—was to teach people how to live in harmony with their natural surroundings, to "bring out the individual in each of us, in our very being."

"To, as Joseph Campbell suggested," he says, "live our joy, live our bliss. That was the crux of my grandfather's message."

Toward the end of the evening, we talk about his grandfather's death, the body lying in state at Taliesin, and Eric's shock—I think that's a good word for it—at how Frank Lloyd Wright looked laid out in his coffin. "My grandfather always seemed like such a big man when he was alive," says his grandson. "But lying there he looked so small."

We settle the check and head for the door. Along the way, Eric volunteers that another part of the "burden" he referred to at the beginning of the night—along with the responsibility of carrying the family name—is the inevitable comparison to his grandfather. When you have Lloyd and Wright strung together, no matter what your first name might be, having the homes and office buildings and churches you design held up to your grandfather's standard is bound to occur.

"People want to see how you measure up," Eric says.

And, I ask, in his own opinion, how does he measures up?

"Pretty well," he says, smiling. "Actually, as I said, even though he was toughest on those he was closest to, I have a feeling my grandfather would have been proud of me."

I spoke with Eric Lloyd Wright from his home in Los Angeles one morning in August 2018. He remembered our dinner in Milwaukee and was happy to talk.

"I'm eighty-eight now and pretty much retired," he said. "I still do some advising on projects when they involve work by either my grandfather or my father. But I'm in good health. The Wright genes are still strong."

He said neither of his two sons had gone into architecture. One is a musician and the other a landscape contractor. "I'm the last of the Lloyd Wrights in architecture," he said, "unless one of my cousin's children is an architect, in which case I don't know about it."

I asked him if he thought the people of Wisconsin had warmed up to his grandfather. "Oh yes, absolutely," he said. "I base that on the response I have had from people since Monona Terrace got up and running." Monona Terrace is a meeting and convention center in Madison that was first proposed by Frank Lloyd Wright in 1938. The Dane County Board rejected the proposal by a single vote. It opened for business almost sixty years later. "That building has had a huge effect on how the people of Wisconsin regard my grandfather."

Eric, who was not involved in the adaptation of his grandfather's original design, sounded genuinely pleased by the upgrade to his grandfather's reputation in Wisconsin. He was always saddened by the relationship between the state and its celebrated native son.

"I think it would make him happy to know that people appreciate his work," Eric said. "I think he probably would have been pleased with the way the building turned out, although he was very hard to please. His expectations were always sky high."

# PART

3

# THE DARK SIDE OF PARADISE

Jerry Boyle for the defense. Photo courtesy of Marna Boyle.

So I took Charles Kuralt's advice, quit my less-than-glamorous grunt job at CBS News, and got a job with a newspaper, the *Daily Record*, in suburban New Jersey. It paid $12,500 to start and probably $12,750 two years later. My first assignment was to write obituaries, ranging from a sweet Italian grandma who stood at the stove each Sunday for fifty-five years and made a vat of homemade spaghetti sauce to a retired petroleum industry analyst who was an expert on the subject of tertiary recovery of oil. Though I was the lowest of the low on the newsroom's totem pole, I liked that job a lot. Every obit was an opportunity to write the story of someone's life. Whether they were experts at marinara sauce or oil drilling made no difference to me. I had a hyperactive imagination in those days—today it's just active—and the local folks were no less inspiring to me than Mohandas Gandhi or Madame Curie.

After I mastered this assignment, I rose exactly one rung on the ladder, to police reporter. The triple cool thing about this job—other than the fact that I had maybe twenty-five cop shops to cover—was the fact that I had a two-way radio installed in my car. "KRQ five-six-nine, thirty-seven to remote one," I announced, dozens of times a day. Immediately the city editor would come on the line—he was listening to the police radio—and tell me where to go. I was "thirty-seven" (maybe I was the thirty-seventh person who held the job?) and that got me all puffed up with the pride of my profession. I was Woodward and Bernstein rolled into one, only I was investigating a missing gallon of chocolate mint chip at the local Baskin-Robbins rather than the Watergate Hotel. It didn't matter to me. I felt important.

It was a grisly beat, particularly at first, but my initial revulsion vanished in the romance of "The Front Page." I covered deadly car crashes ("fatals" to us tough guys), shootings, armed robberies, drownings (where I learned to coat my nostrils with Vicks VapoRub to combat the stench), murders, the occasional Jersey mob job, and more drug busts than I can possibly remember. I spent at least ten hours a day in the company of cops, some of whom were astronomical assholes (a uniform will do that to some people) and others who were genuinely good people willing to show me the ropes.

Aside from just gathering the cop news, there was a diplomatic dimension to the job: it was my responsibility to get a picture of whoever ended up dead on my "run." Doing this usually meant approaching the family of the deceased at a time when they were distraught. It was distasteful at first, but, like everything else, you got used to it. I developed my own personal pitch, which was a cross between a clergyman (compassionate, consoling, respectful) and a cop (authoritative).

It seems odd and even stupid to say so all these years later, but it started out as such fun. Sure, the subject matter was dreadful, but these were "stories," and the word "story" seemed to have an implied element of fiction about it. If you were going to make it on the police beat, you had to distance yourself emotionally from the human side of things. So I did that—with enthusiasm. At least until I got my head snapped and started to grow up, which took quite a little while.

I was at work one Sunday afternoon when a story came across the Associated Press wire. It was a report of a drug deal gone bad in Colorado. The reason we were interested was that a nineteen-year-old guy was murdered and he was from our New Jersey neighborhood. The story was already twelve hours old when it made it to me, but those were the days before the internet and the never-ending news cycle. My boss told me to call the cops in Colorado, get the scoop, then go to the victim's home and speak with the family. Oh, and let's not forget that my editor said, "Get a picture or don't bother coming back."

I drove to the victim's home in a suburb called Mendham. It was a leafy, tree-lined street, and his parents' place was a meticulously manicured minimansion—a lot nicer than the homes of most of the drug victims I had visited. I went to the front porch and rang the bell. I wasn't nervous. I had done this dozens of times.

A very proper, handsome, gray-haired lady wearing a bright sweater and plaid skirt with a pair of reading glasses hung around her neck opened the door. I had on a white shirt and tie and had combed my hair carefully. She looked calm and confident and pretty friendly. She looked . . . composed. I thought that was a little odd given what was going on in her life. She stepped out on the porch. She smiled. "Yes?"

I told her my name. I said I was a reporter with the *Daily Record*. I said I hated to interrupt at a *time like this* and I knew it was—at best—inconvenient. She looked a little puzzled but nothing very different from what most people look like when a reporter shows up on their doorstep. But she didn't speak, and, for me, silence was the enemy.

"Of course, we intend to do a story about what happened to your son," I said. "If you could just tell me a little about him—his background, schooling, siblings—I would be very grateful. We want to be sure we have a well-rounded story about his life."

She had gone from composed to confused.

"And if it wouldn't be too much to ask," I picked up, "we would really like to run a picture of your son with the story. You probably have one that you're particularly fond of. We'll run whichever picture you would prefer." I was done with my pitch. This was the point—I know it sounds odd—where the grieving family would often invite me inside. They always figured that the reporter knew more than the cops had told them. They were, understandably, desperate for information.

She did not invite me in, but she spoke.

"Are you telling me that my son is dead? Is that what you are saying?" Her voice was cracking, and she was having difficulty drawing breath. A mixture of confusion and horror darkened her face, like a cloud suddenly crossing in front of the sun.

I had heard the expression—it was just that, a colorful turn of phrase—"knee knocking" all my life. But I had never experienced the actual physical sensation. Now I did. I realized that I had just broken the news to this nice lady, someone's mother, that her son had been murdered. And my bony knees—quite literally and loud enough to hear the repetitive thud like a heartbeat in my ears—began to knock uncontrollably. I thought I would collapse in a heap right then and there.

"Are you telling me that my son is dead?" she asked again, and now her voice was shrill and shaking. The bewilderment in her eyes had turned to anguish. I had seen that look only one other time in my life—on the face of the mother of a friend of mine after her son had been killed.

On this day, at this moment, I found my voice, but barely. "I'm sorry. I assumed you knew, since it happened yesterday. I think you will want to call the police." And with that I wrote down the number of the Colorado cop I had talked to and passed it to her. She took the piece of paper from my trembling fingers, then turned and walked back into that beautiful home, which I was pretty sure would never be the same again.

That was the only time in my lengthy career in the news business that I ever told someone that a loved one had been murdered. It had a lasting effect on me: never again would I think of what I was doing as the pursuit of "stories." The word "story" had always had an element of fiction about it. But there was nothing imaginary about the things we were putting in the newspaper. It was as real as real could be, and, aside from the deceased, there were whole lives and families left in the wake of these deaths that were forever altered.

I stayed in the news business for a long time—and much of it I loved—after that knee-knocking day. But that experience took something out of me, or maybe put something necessary into me. Like my sometime mentor Charles Kuralt at CBS, I lost a lot of my lust for the dark side of reporting. That's not to suggest that I stopped then and there writing about life's seamy side. No, I continued to do that because it was part of the job—but I like to think that I did it with more maturity and empathy.

There were two *stories* in particular during my tenure as a reporter and editor at the *Milwaukee Journal*—one that I covered personally and a much bigger one that I oversaw coverage of—that eventually extinguished my appetite for daily journalism altogether.

I'll tell you about those—and some other dark, sordid Wisconsin tales—in the chapters that follow.

# TRAGEDY WITHOUT REASON

## The Eerie Calm of John Norton

As a teenager, I read Truman Capote's *In Cold Blood*, the story of mass murder in a most unlikely place, the small farming community of Holcomb, Kansas. What somehow made the story even more horrifying and incomprehensible was the fact that the murders took place against a background of lush, wide-open prairie and the comfort and safety of small-town living. Of course it was different from the Norton murders, which took place on a dairy farm in Barron County, Wisconsin. In that instance, the four victims weren't executed by a pair of psychotic strangers passing through. They were murdered by a person near and dear to them—their husband and father, his motives inexplicable.

I was sent to the scene of the Norton murders right after the news broke in May 1979. I returned a week after the dead had been buried. The only thing left was a painful array of questions that would never be answered.

In a violent, imperfect world, there are some places where murder and mayhem actually seem to fit. But the John Norton farm is not one of those places.

The land that Norton and his family farmed south of Chetek is all gently undulating green hills and rich pasture populated by black-and-white cows. The Red Cedar River is just around the bend, and when the sun shines, kids who resemble Huck Finn finish farm chores and then swim and fish and dream on its idyllic banks.

For people who live around here and knew the Nortons—a peaceful, friendly, Christian family who both worked and prayed hard—it is never going to be quite the same again. No one knows why John Norton snapped, and they never will.

At 3:16 a.m. on Friday, June 15, the phone rang at the Barron County Sheriff's Department. The conversation was taped:

DISPATCHER: Sheriff's Department.
NORTON: This is John Norton, Route 1, Chetek.
DISPATCHER: Uh, huh.
NORTON: You gotta come over and pick up some bodies.
DISPATCHER: Pick up some bodies?
NORTON: Right.
DISPATCHER: What kind of bodies?
NORTON: Dead bodies. (A brief pause.) This is no fault of God or His church. I was a coward. My wife and my children were cowards. I couldn't bear to see them live that way.

During the next five minutes, Norton, 42, a dairy farmer who lived here for nine years, described to the police dispatcher what he had done. With no hint of remorse in his voice—with no emotion whatsoever—he reported that he had killed his wife, Maxine, 40, and their three children: Jim, 14; Dan, 8; and April, 6.

He said he had struck each of them in the head with a hammer as they slept—"so they wouldn't know what hit 'em"—then shot them one by one with a deer rifle.

Calmly, painstakingly, Norton told the dispatcher how to find his farm, where to find his calves in the white barn near the house and the cattle in the pasture. There was money to pay the bills, he said, and all legal matters would be handled by the Kostner and Kostner law firm in Bloomer.

Then Norton said that he was going to shoot himself. The dispatcher, who already had a car headed for the farm, asked him to hold on because he needed more details. Norton very deliberately repeated the directions to the farm and the whereabouts of the cattle.

DISPATCHER: John, why are you doing this?
NORTON: Because I'm a coward and they're cowards. Because we're church people. I mean, we were to church all the time. We failed God.

The dispatcher asked Norton if he had relatives in the area. Norton said his parents were dead, and anyway, he didn't want his other relatives to know what he had done. They talked a little while longer.

DISPATCHER: It's not going to do any good to kill yourself.
NORTON: Why, it sure is.
DISPATCHER: What are you going to accomplish, John?
NORTON: I'm not going to accomplish anything now with all these dead people.

The conversation covered more details about the law firm that would handle the disposition of the farm.

NORTON: OK, now the reason I done this wasn't the fault of anyone but myself. I couldn't raise 'em right and I couldn't do right with 'em.

And once again he told the dispatcher just exactly where the cattle were located, and he urged the dispatcher to "write that down," lest he forget.

NORTON: Now, that's all you have to know. Goodbye.

A sheriff's deputy arrived at the farm a few minutes after the phone conversation concluded. Norton, who shot himself in the head, was dead on the kitchen floor. His wife and children, victims of the hammer and gun, were dead in their bedrooms, just as he said they would be.

"And the cattle and calves," said Barron County sheriff Wally Larson, "were exactly where he said they'd be."

The Reverend Norman Phillips is pastor of the Advent Christian Church of Chetek, the Norton family's church. He has been trying to wrap his mind and heart around this tragedy.

"I talked to a friend down in Illinois who has had experience with cases like this, and we tried to find a clue, a hint, that this was going to happen," said Phillips. "But we can't find any."

Phillips said the Norton family had just returned from a vacation to Yellowstone, and by all accounts, it had been a good one.

Said Phillips: "John was a good Christian, a very sincere man and an emotional man. He had times of depression but it never incapacitated him. I like the kind of person who calls on you when he needs help, and that's the kind of person John was. He wouldn't let things brew for weeks—he'd call."

Phillips said Norton's statement on the telephone—that he was a coward and had somehow failed his God—was unfathomable. He said the Advent Christian Church believed in the literal return of Jesus Christ and that people were put on earth to "prepare His kingdom."

Phillips said Norton, like most farmers, was in debt. And although he apparently was able to pay his bills, Norton had a harder time than most dealing with the notion of "owing anybody."

Enough to drive him to kill his family and take his own life?

"No," said Phillips.

Several times, Phillips referred to Norton as a "fine husband and father, a man who never abused his wife or children." On the evening prior to the murders, in fact, Norton had taken his children fishing on the Red Cedar River.

"John Norton was an excellent father," said Phillips. "In fact—and I know this probably sounds a little odd—I could have used him in a sermon as an illustration of what a good father should be."

Phillips said the Norton murders have left a deep scar on the collective psyche of the church. It will take time to heal, he said. "It's frustrating when you can't put your finger on a reason for this kind of tragedy," said Phillips. "But like the rest of the church, I'm going to have to learn to live with it."

Sheriff Wally Larson said what so many others had said after the carnage at the Nortons' farm.

"We're living out in the country with farmers and cows. We don't expect these things to happen out here. I listened to the tape a hundred times, looking for something that may have indicated that John Norton didn't murder his family and kill himself. I suppose I didn't want to believe that he could have done something like that. But at this point, I'm thoroughly convinced that he did.

"It is hard to figure. I mean, the things he said on the tape—from everything I've been able to gather—just weren't true. Everybody said he had marvelous kids and he was a marvelous father. He said he wasn't doing enough for the church. But everybody said he probably did more for his church than 98 percent of all the churchgoers in the world. It just doesn't make sense."

Did the investigation lead Larson to believe the murders and suicides were planned?

"That's very hard to know," the sheriff replied. "But all the details on the tape and arrangements with the law firm and such make me think that it was not all planned that night. It may have been something he was thinking about for a while. All I know is that it was bad news."

◇

The sun was beating down on the Norton farm last Wednesday morning. John Johnson, Norton's half brother from Minneapolis, and Kermit DeVoss, a brother-in-law from Illinois, were out in the yard. They had inherited the torturous task of cleaning up.

Johnson said a neighbor was probably going to buy the farm. The cattle and machinery would be sold at auction.

"We're holding up," Johnson volunteered.

Johnson said John Norton was born in Menomonie. His parents were divorced when he was a boy and his mother remarried. He said Norton drove a truck in Eau Claire for a time, then farmed over in a place called Boyceville before moving here nine years ago.

In the past five years—since both men had children about the same age—they had begun to see more of one another. Johnson and DeVoss said they had both seen the Nortons in April, and the family seemed happy and healthy.

Said Johnson: "I don't know what happened. We heard that John had become forgetful lately, that he was losing his memory. It makes you think that maybe he had a brain tumor and maybe that's what's responsible for this. You'd like to believe something like that, that it was physical. But we'll never know. He shot himself in the head. There wasn't any autopsy."

Two miles northeast of the Norton home sits the Schofield farm. Art and Ruth Schofield were the Nortons' closest friends. They attended the same church and have two boys the same age as Jim and Dan Norton.

"Everybody wants to make John Norton out to be an oddball," said Ruth, her voice cracking, "but he wasn't. He was a very strong, gentle Christian man and a good friend. But he must've had something bothering him over the years. I don't believe it was anything financial. John was milking thirty-three cows and sending thirty-nine hundred pounds of milk every other day. He was doing a tremendous job. I don't think there's another farmer around here doing as well."

Mrs. Schofield said she and her husband had stopped at the Norton farm on Tuesday evening before the tragedy. Her husband's uncle and a close friend of John Norton's, Clayton Garner, had been killed several days earlier in a farming accident. The Schofields had stopped to pick up some food that Maxine Norton had prepared.

"John seemed fine," said Mrs. Schofield. "He had just put new fans in the barn and fixed a broken manure bucket. He was just doing his chores."

About three hours after Norton killed his family and himself, the sheriff arrived at the Schofield farm. He told them what had happened, played the tape recording, and asked if that was Norton's voice. Art Schofield said yes, that was John.

Mrs. Schofield said: "Then Art said he had to go right over and milk John's cows. Our son Eddie got up and asked where he was going. Eddie wanted to know why and my husband said he would tell him later.

"By the time he got to the barn, Eddie was asking why again and finally Art told him. I'll never forget how Eddie just sat there on a milk can holding his head in his hands. It's so hard to believe that the kids won't be coming over anymore and they won't be going to school in the fall or that Maxine and I won't sit down and drink coffee and go shopping at Rice Lake.

"Some things in life just don't make any sense. This is one of them."

I stopped at the Barron County Sheriff's Department after I left the Norton farmhouse that day. I picked up a cassette tape of John Norton's conversation with the dispatcher. I had a four-hour drive back to the office, and I must have played that tape a dozen times. John Norton's voice was eerily calm. He might as well have been calling the local farm supply store to see if a tractor part had arrived. I had seen murder scenes before, though never one this grisly. But the tape was the part I couldn't shake: the disconnected-yet-detailed voice directing traffic to and around the farm. He was so concerned about the cows. I guess he figured that everyone else would be gone. Better to tend to the living.

We've all listened to a song that, for whatever reason, we just can't get out of our heads. That's the way it was with that tape. I kept replaying it involuntarily in my mind for a month. There was no on/off switch. It played over and over and over whenever it pleased. Finally the loop stopped. Whenever I think of the Norton murders, which I do occasionally, I'm reminded of something my mother used to ask me when I had covered a particularly ugly story: "Do you think this is really a good job for a man with a college degree?" I used to laugh when she said that. After I witnessed the aftermath of John Norton slaughtering his wife and children, I thought it was a reasonable question.

# THE PAIN OF NEVER KNOWING

## Mary Wegner

I distinctly remember a conversation with a young colleague at the *Milwaukee Journal* in the early 1990s: We had been investigating a case that involved some unpleasant characters. There had been veiled threats made against a reporter on the story and me as managing editor. It was not unusual to be confronted—or at least warned—by one of the bad guys. In fact, it was a badge of honor.

"But aren't you afraid?" my young colleague asked. I said I wasn't, because I had been warned too many times to count and nothing had ever happened. They were just people feeling the heat, I said, and aside from one instance—a sit-down with some IRA thugs in Belfast who told me that if I didn't write nice things it would go badly for me—most of the threats I had received in my career were idle.

Mary Wegner (*left*) and her daughter Laurie Depies, who vanished without a trace in 1992. Photos courtesy of Mary Wegner.

"Is there anything you're afraid of?" my colleague asked me.

Of course there were a lot of things that I was fearful of, but one in particular came immediately to mind. "I'm afraid that something might happen to one of my children," I said. "I don't think I could survive it."

Mary Wegner has lived that nightmare for twenty-seven years. Her daughter Laurie Depies vanished without a trace after leaving work at the Fox Valley Mall on the night of August 19, 1992. I have kept in touch with Mary on and off since her daughter's disappearance. She is always gracious but the conversations are always tough. One of those conversations took place in the summer of 2000.

It was last June or it might have been July, Mary Wegner was saying. It was last summer or was it two summers ago? She wasn't exactly sure.

Anyway, the exact month or year didn't really matter. What mattered was that they found the remains of a woman near Amherst Junction, and after all these agonizing years, she thought it just might be her daughter Laurie Depies, who disappeared one summer night in 1992.

She drove there—to a wayside near the Tomorrow River, not far from some railroad tracks—to a secluded spot where they found the bones of some poor soul. She thought it seemed oddly promising. The wayside was not far from Highway 10, which seemed a logical spot to dispose of a person who lived in Appleton and whose car had been found in a parking lot at her boyfriend's apartment in Menasha. Also, though she was quick to say that this wasn't what ultimately compelled her, she remembered that not long after Laurie's disappearance a psychic predicted that her body would be found by a river near some railroad tracks. So the pieces were more or less in place.

But the real reason she drove to Portage County, where she knew that she was likely inviting another episode of emotional whiplash, was, as she says over a cup of coffee, "because you just never know."

So she went to see. The authorities sent the remains to the State Crime Laboratory in Madison, where they would determine if a DNA match existed based on blood samples taken from Mary and from Laurie's biological father. And then Mary Wegner waited.

"The waiting is hard," she says. "You use up an awful lot of mental and emotional energy. It's draining. Until you get an answer, you're pretty much an emotional wreck."

When the answer finally came it was, once again, negative. The remains were not those of Laurie Depies.

"It probably sounds weird but, you know, I was hoping it was Laurie," her mother says, clearly wondering if I can possibly understand that statement. "So we could put it to rest. After all these years, you want to know."

"After all these years"—it will be eight years this August 19—the police still don't have a clue what happened to Laurie. All anybody knows is that she left her job at a local mall after work on August 19, 1992, and drove to her boyfriend's apartment complex. The next morning they found her car parked in the lot. Nobody—at least nobody who's talking—has seen or heard from her since. She was twenty at the time.

"She just disappeared," says her mother. "After all this time, there's nothing new."

I met Mary Wegner after Laurie's disappearance and wrote a column about a parent's worst nightmare. We met at a Perkins restaurant on that morning, as we did again last week. There was a difference between those two visits: Back then there seemed to be a picture of Laurie Depies on every telephone pole and in every shop window in Wisconsin. On this day—eight years later—like most of Mary's hopes, the posters are long gone.

I came across that original column a few weeks ago. I hadn't heard anything about Laurie Depies in a long time. I wanted to call Mary Wegner, but I hesitated. She had been through hell and beyond, and I figured she would have no interest in resurrecting bad memories. I certainly didn't want to be cruel.

"Actually, I like talking about her," Mary says, sipping her coffee and nibbling on a cookie. "Talking brings her back. I mean, she's with me all the time, but talking about her like this puts life in the images."

Under the circumstances, Mary Wegner seems to be doing remarkably well. She's fifty-three now but doesn't seem to have aged a day since our last cup of coffee. She laughs easily but, as she's quick to point out, she also cries more often and with less provocation. Her emotions exist closer to the surface.

Nonetheless, she keeps herself busy with her husband, Andrew Wegner; her daughter Julie; five children she inherited through her second marriage; and a new grandchild. She retired from her job three years ago and has developed an avid interest in genealogy.

"Part of the reason I've gotten so interested in family history is because of Laurie," Mary volunteers. "In a way, I'm documenting her life. I don't want her to be forgotten."

If she has a mission inspired by her daughter's disappearance, it's to preach the gospel of openness, to encourage family and friends and total strangers to reach out to the people they love and tell them. If she has regrets regarding her relationship with Laurie, it's that there was so much left unsaid.

Of course, I assure her, what parent of any young adult doesn't feel estranged from a kid trying to establish independence? It's part and parcel of the process. She agrees.

"But she was *such a stranger* at the time she disappeared," Mary says. "I didn't know enough about her life. She wouldn't let me in her life. It reminded me of when I was a stay-at-home mom and the girls first went to school all day. It was a big deal when they came home, and I would always ask, 'What happened today?' and they would just say, 'Nothing' or 'Not much.' They started to have their own lives and their own secrets separate from me. It's hard for a mother to take. That's the same way I felt when Laurie vanished. I wasn't a big enough part of her life."

The police still think there's a small chance that Laurie might have just walked away. Mary has a hard time believing that. She is convinced that her daughter is dead. Nonetheless, as she phrases it, she "keeps a little window open" in her psyche for the possibility that Laurie is still alive.

"What nags at my heart most, I guess, is that Laurie never got to develop her talents. She never really knew what she was good at. She was still very much trying to figure out what she was going to do with her life. She would be twenty-eight today, turning twenty-nine on September 17.

"You know, I would give anything to know what she looked like at twenty-eight. I mean, how her features developed and, well, everything about her. Would she still be so rebellious? Would she have had her belly button pierced? Who would she have married? Where would she live? Would she have children by now? Oops, here I go." She puts her coffee cup down, grabs a napkin, and dabs a moist eye.

"It's as if her life just stopped at twenty. It's funny but when I dream about her nowadays—and I dream about her often—she is always a teenager or younger."

The mystery of Laurie Depies's disappearance is just that. Occasionally the police get a tip or somebody overhears somebody at a bar who claims to know something. But it never checks out.

For her part, Mary Wegner remains convinced that somebody knows something, and not necessarily the person who abducted Laurie. Her daughter had a circle of maybe twenty friends with whom she spent a lot of time. One of those kids—none of whom Mary has any contact with anymore—knows something about what happened to Laurie.

"I'm absolutely convinced that somebody knows something," she says. "They may not know exactly what happened that night, but they might. Or they know something that led up to whatever happened that night and it just hasn't come out before. If I had those twenty friends in front of me, here's what I'd say: 'Can't someone come forward and tell me what happened? I'm sure you know how much I'm still hurting after all these years.' That's what I'd say."

She stares at the restaurant table and turns her cookie clockwise around the plate. She is taking a minute to regain her composure. She dabs at her eyes with the napkin again. She looks at the stranger on the other side of the table.

"Do you think that's too much to ask?"

I have spoken with Mary Wegner a number of times since Laurie disappeared in 1992 at age twenty. We had our most recent conversation on September 10, 2018, a breathtakingly beautiful Indian summer day, just a week before what would have been Laurie's forty-seventh birthday. We spoke for an hour.

In so many ways Mary leads the life of a typical seventy-one-year-old woman making the most of retirement. She travels—to Ireland, England, Germany, and just this summer a river cruise down the Rhine—and spends as much time as possible with her grandchildren. She dearly loves her home now in Amherst Junction and the beauty that surrounds it. If I didn't know better, it would all seem so nice and normal.

But if I've learned anything from my periodic conversations with Mary over more than two decades, it's that you build your own "normal" with whatever material is available. "What else can you do?" she asks. "The only thing to do is carry on as best you can."

A few years ago, when a prison inmate named Larry Dewayne Hall confessed to abducting and murdering Laurie, Mary allowed herself to think that some sort of closure was in sight. But that all dissolved when, despite indications to the contrary, the cops decided Hall was making it up. "He was a wannabe serial killer," said Kyra Schallhorn of the Wisconsin Department of Justice. Mary wasn't so sure. "He had been in the area around the time Laurie disappeared, and he had her name on a piece of paper in his van," she said. When the police decided not to bring him to Wisconsin and let him take them to where he supposedly hid her body, Mary descended— for a while—into the pit of despair. And she was a little angry too.

"I think the police have just thrown in the towel," she said. "When they sent two big shots from the Department of Justice up to see us, and they told us they thought Larry Hall was the one, well . . ." Her voice trailed off.

She said that she had hoped to go to the prison in North Carolina where Hall was held. "I wanted to sit down and talk with him myself," she said. Her voice was very calm. "I wanted to speak to him not as someone seeking vengeance but as a mother wanting to know what had happened to her child. You have children. You know what I mean, right?" Right, I said. Honestly, though, the thought of calmly sitting face-to-face with someone who may have murdered my child only made me think of how I would want to murder the murderer right then and there. But I didn't say that.

I told her she was a remarkable person in my humble estimation. (What could I possibly know about such torment? Nothing.) She is no hero, she assured me. "I go through periods of depression. I question what I might have done differently in my relationship with my daughter. But in the end I've come to realize that there's nothing I can do for Laurie now. Stiff upper lip, you know? I suppose that's the English stoicism in my background."

The conversation paused for a long, pregnant moment. Then she said it's not that she's totally stoic or that her nerve endings have numbed after all these years. She's simply developed ways to compartmentalize and cope. "In my case, I've built a little glass house in my mind and heart," she said. "Laurie is inside that house. Most of the time the shades are drawn. But then something happens, something random, and it triggers a memory or feeling about Laurie. And that's when I pull the shades up and I peek inside and see her."

Does peeking inside cause pain? Or does it resurrect hope?

"I think I'm past the point of hope," she said. "I used to have these fleeting thoughts, almost dreams, that one day Laurie would call me on the telephone or just walk into the yard. I had those thoughts for a long while. Now I consider them frivolous and I don't allow them. Those thoughts are gone."

# Living with the "Enemy"

## Bill Fero

I can't remember exactly how I first heard about Bill Fero. I think it was when I was writing a series of articles for the *Milwaukee Journal* about the resettlement of Vietnamese refugees in Wisconsin. It was not all open arms. One day I was sent to Manitowoc to do a story about "growing tensions"—hostility would be a better word—that had surfaced between local fishermen and the Vietnamese refugees. It was an ugly scene. For the locals, fishing was mostly entertainment. They didn't need the catch to survive. The Vietnamese were "meat hunters," I remember a fisherman from Two Rivers telling me. They needed the fish to feed their families. Eventually, as time passed, the old-timers and the new arrivals made a passable peace. But there was a rough period of adjustment.

It was during that time that someone told me about Bill. He was a guy from Whitewater who had served in Vietnam and paid a dear price—he lost both legs. Now he was back in his hometown and had opened his home to a revolving cast of Vietnamese refugees. As I was to learn, it was an arrangement that benefited both parties.

Bill Fero watched as the tiny Vietnamese girl, virtually hidden behind the box of Lucky Charms she carried, padded across the kitchen floor. The child paused for a fraction of a second, glanced at Fero to see if he was watching, then dropped her cereal box and opened a drawer in one motion. There was shiny silverware inside, and her eyes opened wide with wonder.

"No, no, baby," the man said softly to the child. And she stepped back, bent at the waist to retrieve her box, smiled at the man, and wobbled off.

Fero spoke softly: "I used to wonder if I had to keep these people near me—this is the second refugee family I've sponsored—just to keep from hating them." He watched the child turn a corner. "Now they're like family. You know, there's nobody who could remodel a house by himself, not even with a good pair of legs."

Bill Fero, thirty, does not have a good pair of legs. He has hardly any legs at all. What's left are two stumps that end just above the knee. He lost them in Vietnam. That seems like a long, long time ago.

"I volunteered to go in 1971," Fero recalled. "I was part of a demolition team that used to be dropped in at night to blow up roads and bridges." One night in the summer of 1971, Fero and twenty other American soldiers met in a clearing to map strategy. The Vietcong must have been tipped off, he figures, because the rendezvous site was mined with explosives.

"All I remember is a loud ringing and a flash of light," said Fero, who was tossed fifty feet by the blast. He counts himself among the fortunate: eighteen of his colleagues were killed.

After years recuperating in hospitals from Southeast Asia to Milwaukee—and receipt of a Purple Heart from General William Westmoreland—Fero set out to start life over. For a while he wandered around the US. Then, about two years ago, he bought a small farm outside Whitewater, where he grew up.

As he tells it, soon afterward a local minister appeared on his doorstep. There was a Vietnamese refugee family due to arrive in Whitewater any day. The preacher wondered if Bill, the man who left his legs in Vietnam, had room for the refugees in his farmhouse. "I knew he must have been sent by my aunt," Fero remembered. "I told him I'd have to think about it."

It wasn't that Fero, like some of the other veterans he knew, held the Vietnamese responsible for his misfortune. On the contrary, he sympathized with the plight of the refugees fleeing their homeland, and he was not particularly proud of the US government's role over there.

What made Fero hesitate, or so it seemed, was the unsettling prospect of taking responsibility for a refugee family. He was afraid. Since he lost his limbs, Fero had learned to rely on others. If he agreed to sponsor the refugees, the burden of reliance would rest with him.

There was precious little time to think about it. The Swan family— a husband, wife, and two children—arrived in a matter of days. Fero decided to take them in. Part of the wave of Vietnamese "boat people," they had been on the sea for forty-two days seeking a friendly port. They shared Fero's farmhouse for five months before joining relatives in California.

"It was a struggle for the first three months," says Fero, who works on the assembly line at General Motors in Janesville. There were considerable cultural adjustments to make on both sides.

"Like I wasn't used to their fish sauce and cooking," he said, laughing. "When they butcher a chicken they use everything. I mean *everything*. I came home from work one night and there was soup on the stove. It smelled good, so I took a bowl. I stuck my spoon in there and pulled out a shriveled chicken leg and whatever. I didn't care for that much."

He also remembers his surprise when one of the children came down with a headache and, instead of prescribing aspirin, the child's mother opted to feed her boiled nightcrawlers as a remedy. The child recovered. Worms notwithstanding, things went well for Fero and the Swan family. And when they left in the summer of 1979, he offered to sponsor another. The Tran family has been with him ever since.

While the Tran family learns something about the day-to-day realities of life in this country from their sponsor, Fero feels that he, too, has learned from the Vietnamese. He has also learned something about his friends, he says.

"I've found out who my real friends are. Some others, who I thought were my friends, won't come here anymore because of them. That's just wrong."

Like all human beings, Fero said, there are limits to the refugees' resilience. Sometimes homesickness and a sense of displacement seem to overwhelm them. There are periods of intense depression. It happened recently with the Tran family.

"There was a period there when they just sat and stared," he said. "And Mrs. Tran just cried and cried and cried. They feel desperately lonely and worry about what's happened to their families. If there's a flood in Texas or an earthquake in California, we can call on the telephone and find out what's happened. But you can't call Hong Kong and say, 'Did a boat [from Vietnam] just come in?'"

Fero, who is waiting for his third Vietnamese family to arrive, said he does the best he can to help the refugees through the rough times. And through their reliance on him, the refugee families have helped Fero regain the sense of self-confidence that responsibility instills. They also help combat the loneliness that Bill Fero himself sometimes feels.

Toward the end of our conversation, Fero is sitting in his wheelchair with a five-month-old baby—Lien Cap Kim—in his arms. He looks like any proud father rocking his daughter to sleep. It is a priceless picture.

"They are better than a pair of legs for me," he said. "They are my family."

Bill Fero still lives in Whitewater, though he spends a good portion—months—of each year in Vietnam, frequently shepherding supplies to a needy hospital in Ho Chi Minh City. He continues to heal by sharing his land and his life with Vietnamese people in need.

# THE TRUTH WILL OUT

## The Short, Unhappy Life
## of Emmanuel Dannan

The telephone at the Marquette County Sheriff's Office picks up on the first ring. I tell the dispatcher that I am looking for directions to the Greenwood Presbyterian Cemetery. "I'll bet you're going to visit the grave of the boy who wouldn't tell a lie," says the guy at the other end of the line. "How did you know that?" I ask, a tad taken aback. "Oh, we get a lot of visitors to that boy's grave," says the deputy. "Seems like more and more lately."

I drive south on Highway 22 from Montello until I come to Highway B. I turn left and immediately see the tiny, well-tended graveyard on the south

The gravesite of Emmanuel Dannan—
"The Boy Who Would Not Tell A Lie"—
at a small cemetery south of Montello.
Truth Day is observed every November
30 in Marquette County in honor of a
boy who valued honesty over his own life.

side of the road. I pull onto the grass in front of the church and park across from the cemetery. There are maybe two hundred headstones scattered in the grass, but it's hard to miss the big block letters carved into a six-foot block of red granite:

## EMMANUEL DANNAN

At the foot of the monument, a bouquet of pink, yellow, and white flowers lies on the ground. Emmanuel Dannan has been dead for 168 years. I wonder aloud, "Who in the world leaves flowers at the grave of a child who died in 1851?"

Don Sprain, who is a philosophical sort, leans back and threads his thick farmer's fingers together behind his head.

"Truth is always a good idea," he says. "Truth never goes out of fashion."

Once upon a time, Marquette County set aside a special day to honor truth. It was called, aptly, Truth Day, and there was a ceremony at Emmanuel Dannan's grave across from the Greenwood Presbyterian Church. There were speeches made and songs sung, and the late F. Rogers Constance composed a poem for the occasion. It concluded:

> He honored truth and died for it
> And the truth did set him free.
> Could God deny such faith to man
> Including you and me?

"The last Truth Day was held on September 14, 1980, and more than two thousand people attended," Fran Sprain remembers. "It was a very special day."

I attended the graveyard ceremony and wrote about that special day back in 1980. After that, every time I raced past the Montello exit on Highway 51, I wondered what became of Truth Day. That's what motivated my trip to the Marquette County Historical Society one summer morning years later to talk to the Sprains.

Emmanuel Dannan was born in 1843, the sixth child of Mary and Benjamin Dannan of Devonshire, England. His family came to Milwaukee in 1846. Within two years, both his parents had died. The boy was adopted by an uncle in 1848, but the uncle, too, died soon thereafter. Emmanuel was placed in the Milwaukee Poor House and was eventually adopted by Samuel W. Norton, a farmer from the Town of Buffalo in rural Marquette County.

According to newspaper accounts at the time, Norton murdered a peddler who was making the rounds of local farms. Emmanuel knew about the killing, and, when the dead man's horse was discovered on the farm and local police got interested, Norton ordered his adopted son to lie about what had transpired.

Emmanuel told Norton over and over again that he would not lie, that his parents had taught him never to tell a lie. Finally, angered by the boy's refusal, the farmer tied the boy's wrists together with rope, tossed one end over a crossbeam in the barn, and stretched Emmanuel to the very top of his tiptoes.

An account of the incident written by the Reverend W. W. Arnett in 1854 said that Norton whipped the boy for more than two hours using a dozen willow switches. Finally, Emmanuel uttered the words, "Pa, I'm so cold," and died.

Newspaper reports about Samuel Norton—he was convicted of first-degree manslaughter and served seven years in prison—said doctors examining the boy's body found "there was not a spot from the armpits to the ankles large enough to place your finger which was not covered with livid welts and broken skin."

The story was forgotten for more than a hundred years until Charlie House, a reporter for the *Milwaukee Sentinel*, happened across an account in an 1853 edition of a local newspaper. In the early 1950s, House resurrected the story and its publication generated interest across Wisconsin. The story inspired the Bittman Monument Company of Milwaukee and the Montello Granite Works to join together and construct a red granite memorial to Emmanuel Dannan's life and his devotion to truth. It was dedicated on the first Truth Day, in May 1954, 103 years after the boy was murdered.

On this sultry summer morning decades later, the Sprains direct me to the Greenwood cemetery on Highway B, south of Montello, the place where Emmanuel Dannan is buried. It is not hard to find.

I park on the south side of the road, across from where two men are moving concrete steps with a backhoe. I walk across the cemetery grass, past the graves of Lucy Belau and Civil War veteran Frederick Opperman of Company 1 of the Seventh Wisconsin Infantry. There, by its lonesome, stands the red granite headstone guarding the grave of Wisconsin's "humblest hero."

EMMANUEL DANNAN

1843–1851

"THE BOY WHO WOULD

NOT TELL A LIE"

*Blessed are they which are persecuted*
*For righteousness' sake:*
*For theirs is the kingdom of heaven.*
*Matt. 5:10.*

"That last Truth Day in 1980 was a success," remembers Fran Sprain, many years later. "After that it just disappeared. I don't know why. It's a shame. It was such a special day."

Nowadays you can buy calendars telling you that almost every day of the year has been anointed Secretary's Day or Sweetest Day or Guacamole Day or—the granddaddy of all these terminally commercial celebrations—National Donut Day on the first Friday in June. It seems like what we really need—particularly at a time when the world is awash in distrust and lying has become an art form—is a day dedicated to truth. It was such a good idea.

If that special day were to be resurrected, says Fran Sprain, the right person to make it happen would probably be Esther Brancel of Endeavor, the new president of the Marquette County Historical Society. I call Esther and ask her if there is any interest in holding another Truth Day.

"I've given it absolutely no thought," she says. "But, come to think of it, I suppose it would be something fine. And I suppose the sooner we do it, the better. I've always been in favor of the truth."

Several years ago, the Marquette County Board passed a resolution setting aside November 30 each year to remember Emmanuel Dannan. There is no formal gathering like back in the 1980s, but county supervisor Kathleen McGwin told me in September 2018 that the board would be discussing the idea of reviving a Truth Day event this fall.

McGwin is a one-person truth squad. For more years than she cares to remember, she has written an annual essay about Emmanuel Dannan— and what he symbolizes—for the *Marquette County Tribune*. She makes regular visits to schools throughout the year telling children about Emmanuel and why remembering his life—168 years after his death—matters. She also hosts a ceremony each November 30 at his gravesite in the Greenwood cemetery.

"This is my first term on the county board," she told me, "but I'm really intent on getting a formal Truth Day reestablished." I would bet on her.

In one of her annual essays, she wrote: "Repeating the story of Emmanuel Dannan brings us a little closer to grace. It reminds us that lives do matter, the truth does matter, and courage comes in many forms. His story gives us a chance to be better people."

# THE BANALITY OF EVIL

## Jerry Boyle and the Defense of Jeffrey Dahmer

Jerry Boyle grew up on the West Side of Chicago in a house with four older brothers. Cultural anthropologists will tell you that in such a tribe the youngest male gets picked on, tormented, teased, and generally treated as low boy on the totem pole, which, of course, he is. In a big, brawling Irish Catholic family, that's just the natural order of things.

One by one, the older Boyle boys were sent away to Campion, a Jesuit prep school in Prairie du Chien, Wisconsin. The day the last brother was packed off was one that young Jerry had looked forward to for a long, long time—liberation day! As it turned out, there was no parade.

"At first I didn't have any idea what came over me," says Boyle, who as a lawyer was involved in some of Wisconsin's most celebrated and notorious criminal cases. "I just felt weird. I was rid of my older brothers and—it's hard to explain—I thought I was going crazy." Years later he realized that he was suffering from a kind of emotional vertigo. "I had never experienced the sensation of loneliness in my life. My brothers were gone and I missed them. I was profoundly lonely. It's physically painful. And I'll tell you this: I never forgot that feeling."

Jerry Boyle was on his way to the American Club in Kohler one afternoon in July 1991 when a TV reporter called him, wanting to discuss a former client: Jeffrey Dahmer. "The cops think he may have murdered fifteen people." Boyle, who had represented Dahmer in a low-profile case a couple of years earlier, thought the idea was ludicrous. "Jeffrey Dahmer?" Boyle asked. "Jeffrey Dahmer couldn't kill a flea. Jeffrey Dahmer is a shy, wimpy guy. He sure as hell isn't dangerous." In truth, when the reporter first uttered Dahmer's name, Boyle had an immediate, almost visceral reaction: "If anything, I thought Dahmer had been murdered. He had all the earmarks of a victim."

Boyle had run into Dahmer at the Milwaukee County Courthouse not long before that July afternoon. The young man was bruised and battered. He told Boyle that somebody had tried to rob him, and when he resisted, the guy beat him to a pulp. He said he was on his way to file a complaint against his attacker. Boyle didn't know what had really happened, but he was pretty sure that Dahmer was lying through his teeth.

"The cops say they took at least eleven human skulls out of Dahmer's apartment," the reporter told him. "I'll call you right back," Boyle told the reporter. Boyle then dialed Jeffrey Dahmer's father, Lionel, at his home in Ohio and repeated what he had just heard. "It was his father who hired me in that first case," said Boyle. "I thought it was better that he heard it from me than the media."

By the time Boyle got back to Milwaukee, Jeffrey Dahmer had voluntarily confessed—in excruciating detail—to the murder and dismemberment of seventeen human beings. The first thing Boyle said to him was, "Jeffrey, you have to tell me what you want." Dahmer replied, "I want to die." Boyle explained that Wisconsin didn't have the death penalty so he couldn't help him with that. Then he explained Miranda rights and search and seizure, but Dahmer said he wasn't interested in pursuing anything along those lines.

"He told me that he would like to kill himself," Boyle remembers, "but that he didn't think he had the guts to do it." Aside from that, Dahmer said he would just like to know why he was such a bad human being.

Said Boyle: "He was the portrait of anguish. He had been living with this obsession—to have sex with a drugged or dead male body—since he was fourteen years old. Part of him was sad because he knew it was over. But I thought another part of him was probably relieved. In any event, he just wanted to cooperate. He told the coppers everything, even things they didn't ask him about."

Dahmer's father arrived in Milwaukee from Ohio. He walked into a meeting room at the jail and hugged his son. "Are you all right?" he asked. Dahmer said yes, he was all right, adding almost inaudibly, "I guess I did some very bad things."

"It was a strange scene," said Boyle, who has three children of his own. "Here was a father and son meeting under the most horrific of circumstances. And there was no emotion. They might as well have been talking about a minor traffic accident."

Later, alone with his client, Boyle told Dahmer that he would have to tell him everything, tell him the whole truth and nothing but the truth, if he was to represent him effectively. Dahmer did just that; he spilled his guts.

"I had defended murderers and even prosecuted a serial killer years before, when I was in the DA's office," Boyle recalled. "Serial killers are mean, cruel, evil. Serial killers lie. Ted Bundy lied all the way to the electric chair. John Wayne Gacy lied. Michael Lee Herrington, the guy I prosecuted for killing and torturing little girls, lied. Dahmer was one sick puppy, but he wasn't even remotely close to the most evil person I had ever represented. And he didn't lie. He was no serial killer. He was possessed."

As they discussed the inferno that Dahmer had created—starting with his first victim at age fourteen—Boyle had an odd flashback to his own childhood, missing his brothers. Dahmer had a lot of twisted fantasies that were completely out of his control. He may or may not have been insane according to the legal definition. But one thing resonated in the oddest way with Jerry Boyle: *Jeffrey Dahmer was a truly lonely man.*

At one point, he asked Dahmer if he ever had a good friend growing up. "No," Dahmer said. Did you ever go to a party with other kids? "No," Dahmer said. Did you ever go to a friend's house? "No." Did you ever go bowling? "No." Did you ever go to a ball game with a bunch of guys? "No," said Dahmer, "never."

"He was the loneliest human soul I had ever come across," said Boyle. "Of course, I never killed anybody when my brothers went off to Campion. But I had a deep-seated, personal understanding of this thing called loneliness."

Anyone who knows Jerry Boyle—I got to know him well over the years—knows that humor is his lifeblood. In the dark recesses of civilized society, where he operated for most of his professional life as both a prosecutor and a defense attorney, humor was his chief coping mechanism.

Boyle remembers that Dahmer got a lot of mail after his arrest. It fell into three basic categories: Sick letters from men who offered themselves to Dahmer as sexual partners, complete with photographs. A raft of letters from religious people who told Jeffrey that it was not too late to save his soul. And a third category that—if you worked in the mailroom of an insurance company—you might call miscellaneous correspondence.

Said Boyle: "One day I took all the mail to him. I told him that I didn't think he should take any time going through the filth that was sent to him, but, in the end, that was his decision to make. He decided to pass on that pile." As for the religious letters, Dahmer wasn't interested, either.

"I picked up a letter from the third pile and I said to him, 'This one would be okay, but under your current circumstances, I don't really think it's worth reading.' I held it up and showed it to him. It was from American Express Travel Services. He actually laughed. It was the only emotion I ever saw from him besides pain and anguish."

This was hardly the most complicated criminal case Jerry Boyle ever tried. After Dahmer confessed to everything with almost total recall, Boyle's only real job was to try to prove that his client was insane at the time he committed his crimes. In the end, largely because of the methodical way in which he went about his madness, the jury rejected the insanity defense. In February 1992, Dahmer was sentenced to fifteen consecutive life sentences at the Columbia Correctional Institution. In late November 1994, he was beaten to death with a pipe by a fellow inmate.

It was a losing proposition for Boyle from the beginning. His client had already confessed to the murders. And yet, Boyle says, the case was fraught with opportunities to screw up. "If I didn't handle it properly," he says, "I could see myself spending the rest of my career defending traffic cases somewhere in Manitoba. I wanted to make sure that this case was tried only once. I wanted everything to be done right."

I wondered if he was ever inclined to turn down the opportunity to defend Dahmer. Yes, of course, Boyle said. But Dahmer's father pleaded with him to represent his son. "Once I was in it, I was in it for keeps. I had given my word. To try and get out of defending Dahmer would have been cowardly. I try never to be a hero, but I try harder every day not to be a coward."

One of Boyle's missions during the Dahmer trial was to spare the friends and families of his client's victims any further heartache. He tried unsuccessfully to get the judge to allow a system where, given the hideous details surrounding each of the murders, the victims would be described not by name but by number. He felt that this would somehow soften the blow for the families, who were a large and emotional presence every day at the internationally televised trial. The prosecution opposed that idea, arguing that it would *"depersonalize"* the victims. Boyle thought *personalizing* them was an unnecessary hardship for the families. The judge rejected that idea.

The courtroom was a macabre place. It was also, in Boyle's view, a very hostile environment. He could see and feel the rage from the parents, siblings, and friends of the victims directed toward the man— him—defending the beast who had murdered and mutilated their loved ones. "That was just natural," said Boyle. "I would have felt the same way toward the defense attorney if I had been in their shoes." Each victim had three or four relatives or friends present in the courtroom every day. "And every day I walked by them and they glared at me," Boyle said.

So he resolved that in this worst of cases, with nerves so taut and raw all around, he would do everything he could to respect the victims and never disrespect their families. He offered to meet with each family and tell them everything they might want to know about how their loved one had died—including information that didn't come out during the trial. "I was willing to tell them as little or as much as they needed to know to find some sense of peace." Several of the families took him up on his offer after the ordeal was over.

"My proudest day as a lawyer was the last day of the Dahmer trial," he says. "We had finished our daily press conference. There was a corridor in the Milwaukee courthouse that I used every day to make my exit. When I turned into the corridor after making my closing argument, I saw the families of Dahmer's victims standing at the opposite end.

"So now I have a decision to make: I can either go down the corridor and meet them, or find another way out. I decide to continue down the corridor, past the people whose loved ones have been murdered and dismembered by my client. And as I pass, each one of them reaches out and touches me—my hand, my sleeve, my arm—and they say, 'God bless you' or 'Thank you.' The victims' families acknowledged that I had played it straight. That was as moving a moment in my professional life as I can remember."

His voice trails off. But he's not quite done. "I believe this is a profession where you are measured by not whether you win or lose, but how you play the game. You can win despite the verdict. A lawyer can be a lawyer in the worst situation in the world and still emerge with his dignity intact."

The seven-month stretch from the night Jeffrey Dahmer was arrested in July 1991 until his sentencing on February 7, 1992, was the low point of my career in journalism. I was the managing editor of the *Milwaukee Journal* during that period, and from the moment I got a call from a friend in the Milwaukee County medical examiner's office early on July 23, the Dahmer case dominated my daily life. As the leading newspaper in the city where the carnage took place, we wanted to know everything about the rampage of Jeffrey L. Dahmer.

Every morning I ran a news meeting with the top editors. For those seven months, Dahmer was Topic A on the day's agenda. As the guy running the daily show, I had to be all Dahmer, all the time. I couldn't let on how I really felt about this story: I hated it. Maybe it was my age (midforties) or the fact that I was a parent and had small kids but— unlike some of my colleagues—I wished that Jeffrey Dahmer had committed his crimes in another city on the other side of the earth. I found the whole thing incredibly distasteful. To start your day with details about body parts in fifty-five-gallon drums and a guy who had to drain the bathtub of chemicals and move body parts in order to take a shower was enough to put me off my feed. Like my friend Charles Kuralt, I didn't have the stomach for this sort of thing anymore.

I was saddened and disgusted by the whole affair. It was chapter after chapter, day after day, detailing the most ghastly examples of human depravity. We devoted each day to unearthing still more disturbing facts and deciding how much gore was too much for the daily paper that landed on Myrtle's doorstep each afternoon. To be clear, I had enthusiastically participated in plenty of sordid stories over the years, especially when I was a young man, but this one made me want to do something else—anything else—for a living.

◇

Months after Dahmer was sentenced, someone at the *Journal* wrote a letter to him—we had never actually talked to the man—asking if he would consent to an interview at Columbia Correctional Institution. Dahmer answered the letter, and his reply landed in my office. He said that he was a little preoccupied with other matters at the moment (murder charges against him were pending in Ohio) and that he was not granting any interviews. But, he added, if things settled down, he might reconsider.

It was oddly polite and a little familiar, more like a letter home from a busy kid at summer camp rather than a serial killer. I remember sitting in my office that day, staring at the handwriting of this supposed monster. The Dahmer case had been our professional preoccupation for months, and yet this single piece of paper was the only remotely personal contact any of us had had with him. I finally concluded that his penmanship reminded me of an elementary school pupil. It was the deliberate, carefully composed work of a boy whose coordination was not yet fully developed.

At the bottom of the page there was a postscript. Dahmer said that he was enclosing a check for $32.50, drawn on his prison checking account, for a six-month subscription to the Sunday *Milwaukee Journal*, of which he was a regular reader. He wondered if we could sign him up. I gave the check to someone in the circulation department, and Jeffrey Dahmer was added to the mail-edition list. Except for the signature on the page—he signed it "Jeff Dahmer"—there was nothing to distinguish it from all sorts of mail that arrived at the newspaper every day. It was absolutely normal, but—given what I knew about the author—it was more than a little chilling.

Six months after Dahmer was sentenced, I was asked to give a speech to a national gathering of medical examiners. They had come to Milwaukee because of the Dahmer case. They were there to discuss, in scientific detail, the clinical challenge of identifying Dahmer's victims from the remains retrieved from his little chamber of horrors. It was obvious that for medical examiners accustomed to autopsying the bodies of everyday murder and suicide victims, a postmortem of the Dahmer case was like attending the Super Bowl.

I told them how we had covered the story and how we had dealt with matters of taste in publication. Toward the end of my half hour, I mentioned the letter from Dahmer and the $32.50 subscription check. I told the audience, too, that I was always troubled by the fact that Dahmer looked so "normal." And when I finally heard him speak at the sentencing—the first time any of us had heard his voice—he sounded like a reasonably intelligent, articulate, remorseful man. The beast seemed hauntingly human.

After my talk, as I gathered my notes on the stage of the Wyndham ballroom, a man approached. I recognized him immediately. It was Robert W. Huntington, a University of Wisconsin pathologist whom I had witnessed testifying in various murder cases around the state. He was tall and serious and had a huge head of white hair that looked like it had been styled by licking his fingers and inserting them in an electrical outlet.

"You seem to be puzzling over all this normalcy surrounding Jeffrey Dahmer," shouted Huntington, whose twangy voice—he was from West Virginia—had only one volume setting, EXTRA LOUD. "Good God, man, haven't you ever heard of the banality of evil?"

I was familiar with that expression. The philosopher Hannah Arendt had applied it to the Nazis. Nonetheless, I hadn't arrived at the point where I considered evil commonplace. I preferred my mass murderers uncommon and abnormal. I didn't like the idea that they might look or act or sound like you and me.

I thought a lot about Professor Huntington's comments after I heard—just after Thanksgiving in 1994—that Dahmer had been murdered. I was thinking about it as I listened to the people who were interviewed by the media. They ranged from "he was a piece of human garbage and he got what he deserved" to the rather stunning words of a family member of one of Dahmer's victims, who said she felt only sympathy for Dahmer's family. I felt certain that it was one of those women who had touched Jerry Boyle's sleeve and said, "God bless you" and "Thank you, Mr. Boyle."

I wondered how a person was supposed to feel when Dahmer, who created his own personal inferno and stoked it with at least seventeen victims, was beaten to death as he cleaned toilets in a prison.

He committed unspeakable crimes but he looked like a couple of guys in my high school. "He wore those really geeky glasses when I first met him," Boyle told me once, "but when he took them off he was a good-looking guy." He was a cannibal, but when he spoke at sentencing, he sounded more pitiful than deranged. He was going to spend what was left of his rotten life in the hellhole that is a maximum security prison—but at least he would have his Sunday newspaper, comics and all.

No matter how many forensic psychiatrists tried to explain him, Jeffrey Lionel Dahmer just didn't add up. And when the murderer himself was murdered, at least for me, a bit player in this production, it was hard to know what to feel.

Jerry Boyle is retired and lives in southeastern Wisconsin.

# PART

# NOT QUITE PLUMB

"I'll tell you another good thing about snake huntin'," said Woody Roberts. "It's never crowded." Photo by Steve Hannah.

After seventy years of plowing this planet, I know very little with certainty. I feel like I ought to know a lot more by now but—maybe because I should have listened more and talked less—I just don't.

That said, here are four things I know for sure:

1. I know about the undeniable power of compounding.
2. I know that if an old septic tank backs up into the drain in the garage, and your tank has a dry well where the liquids are supposed to pass through a baffle plate downhill once it reaches a critical level, it's possible that you have old clay pipe and the roots (or "ruts" as the septic pumpers say in Wisconsin) have jammed up the passage. In which case you might as well replace the clay pipe with PVC because otherwise it's sure as hell going to happen again, and if it happens in the dead of winter you are going to have to get up at 5 a.m. and pour, then ignite, two twenty-pound bags of charcoal on the snowpack over the septic cover just to lower a broom handle with a mirror attached in order to see just what in the world is going on down there. And that truly double-sucks, as the kids say. So replace the clay pipe with PVC and get a good night's sleep.
3. I know that once you hit sixty-five and you are talking with your friends about just exactly when a particular thing happened, you can either Google it or, more conveniently, just add five or ten years to your original estimate.

These three things are critical to navigating your way through life, but they are not anywhere near as important—at least as far as this next set of stories is concerned—as this last one:

4. I definitely know a character when I meet one.

I'm not talking about character in the sense of being especially morally upstanding—though some of my favorite "characters" in this book certainly were. Many of them were kind, selfless, generous, honest, and had humility to spare. But not all of them. Yet most shared other qualities:

big, occasionally loud but sometimes quite quiet, yet always distinctive personalities; an intense interest in or special talent for something, whether it was catching rattlesnakes or frogs, eating more bratwurst at a single sitting than any other person alive, or taking uncommon pride in a fairly common enterprise, like inventing a bobber that could fly halfway across a pond with minimal effort or a little bellows-like contraption that would allow you to place a hard-boiled egg in the plastic saddle and, with one great downward thrust, dispense an egg as soft and smooth as a baby's bottom; or, one of my favorites, build a porta-potty (as the late Virgil Roberts of Sauk City did) that a tornado couldn't tip over, to name just a few. These characters had a gift for living even seemingly small lives in large ways, a visible twinkle in their eyes, and, at least most of them, a certain something that seems to be disappearing these days in the counterfeit culture of social media—hunger for honest-to-God human contact!

And one other thing: They were so obsessed or just plain good at the things they liked to do—so out there, in some cases—that they were, as the drywallers like to say, "not quite plumb," that is, a little off center. In other words, they were not like you and me—or maybe not like you but maybe a little like me. (After all, I spent time trying to find these offbeat characters and then found myself fascinated by the things that fascinated them, which, as my late mother might say, probably excluded me from the ranks of people she deemed "normal.")

One other thing that, like the one-legged Vietnam vet who picked me up hitchhiking and drove a Corvette forty or fifty miles an hour over the speed limit cross-country, is sadly a subject for another time: I believe I am eternally attracted to these offbeat, eccentric characters because I come from a long line of similar creatures (the old takes-one-to-know-one-theory). Many of my own people were—to put it politely—different. And, as a family, both on the Hannah and the Walsh side, we delighted in their differences.

Does that make any sense to all of you "normal" folks? If not, maybe it will once you read a little further.

# "I'M SO HAPPY IT'S JUST TERRIBLE!"

## Woodrow Wilson Roberts

My great friend and next-door neighbor, the late Bill Beach, was always providing me with good column ideas. He knew I was particularly fond of unusual people and also that there was no human distance I wouldn't travel to meet them.

One evening, as he got out of his car, he saw me in the yard and waved me over. He said that the local Optimist Club had an interesting speaker that day. As the local businessmen were spooning their soup, a man walked into the room. He was a big, square-shouldered, red-faced guy with a gray crew cut, wearing a flannel shirt and a pair of bib overalls. He had a burlap sack slung over his shoulder. Without so much as a how-do-you-do, he opened the top of the sack and turned it upside down. Out on the floor of the banquet room spilled three highly agitated rattlesnakes. Bill said the people up front made a move for the rear before the host stepped in—but not too close—and introduced the big man as Mr. Woodrow Wilson Roberts, a full-time farmer and lifelong rattlesnake hunter from Iowa County. It made the Optimists squirm, but it was considerably more entertaining than hearing about the prospects for next season's high school football team.

"You need to meet Woody Roberts," Bill told me that night. "The snakes are pretty tame compared to his personality. He's your kind of guy." So I called Woody and he invited me down to his farm near Arena to talk about his all-time favorite hobby: catching rattlesnakes.

To paraphrase Alfred Lord Tennyson, in spring young Woodrow's fancy lightly turns to rattlesnakes.

"When I'm huntin' snakes, I'm so happy it's just terrible!" says Woody Roberts. The expression on his face sits somewhere between pain and joy when he utters that sentence. "I don't know but I'm just fascinated with snakes. Have been since I was a boy. I like to come up on 'em in the woods and see which way they're layin', see which way their head's turned. Oooooh, it's just my most favorite hobby."

Woodrow Wilson Roberts has been pursuing his most favorite hobby for most of his seventy-eight years. Throughout Iowa County and a ways beyond, Woody is to catching snakes what Willie Mays was to catching flies.

Only his hobby is a most dangerous game.

"I've got no fear of snakes," says Woody, who's been bitten just once in his career. "Only thing I fear is when I let one get away from me. You just can't imagine how awful bad I feel when that happens. Though—and I'm not stuffin' you—they seldom do."

Woody was twelve when he got his first rattlesnake in 1930. The Roberts log farmhouse had twelve people under one roof and money was tight. The bounty on rattlesnakes was fifty cents a head when Woody's dad gave him the green light to hunt them.

"My brother Bert and I went up on that hill over there," he says, pointing to a wooded slope a half mile south of his home. "We saw two of 'em just lyin' there. I said, 'There's a dollar bill on the ground.' We got 'em both. Since then, I never quit."

We talk for a few minutes about snakes Woody has known, about how proud he is of his snake-hunting son Phil—"the most outdoors boy you've ever known"—and how his wife, Jemima, regrettably, just can't abide the sight of snakes. "She's been a good wife all these years," says Woody, the picture of disappointment. "I'd do anythin' if she could learn to love snakes. But she just can't."

I take this moment to tell Woody—offhandedly, because I don't want to come off like some kind of wimp—that I am not all that fond of snakes myself. Woody just smiles.

"But I believe that you're a boy who could *learn* to like snakes," he says, confidently. (I am a boy of forty-seven.) "C'mon, I want to show you a hill where my brother and me caught a two-headed snake once."

After fifteen minutes of hiking, Woody announces—with great volume and even greater animation—that as God is his judge, we are standing on one of the absolute finest rattlesnake hills on Earth. I ask him if this hill has a name to match his enthusiasm. Yes, he says, as a matter of fact it does.

"I call this the Awful Good Snake Hill," proclaims Woody, with great ceremony. Then he points to a rock ledge maybe two feet behind my heels. "And that is where they live."

A moment later, Woody is on his knees in front of the rattlesnake den. He is rhapsodizing about how many snakes are curled up in there, "just back beyond the frost line." He's got his nose practically under the ledge and now he's whistling and jabbing a stick in among the snakes. "I don't know if I can get 'em to come out because it's a little too cold," he apologizes. "But I might be able to get 'em to rattle for you."

After a few minutes of poking and prodding, Woody quits trying to roust the rattlers. He sighs deeply, sadly. It's just a little too chilly on this late April day to get the gang to come out and greet me. He is heartbroken. I am relieved.

"You come back in three weeks—just before Decoration Day—and I'll *gar-un-tee* you plenty of snakes." He is trying to make me feel better, unaware that I already feel better.

Back at the house, Woody brings out pictures of him with rattlesnakes, shows off his practically patented homemade snake tongs, and lets me view one of his prized keepsakes, the skin of a highly poisonous "two-step" snake. "They call it that because when it gets you," he says, cheerfully, "you take two steps back and drop dead."

We shake hands. Once more, he promises we'll get snakes if I come back.

Three weeks later—I'm not sure what possesses me—I take Woody up on his invitation to try again. This time, when I pull up to his house, Woody is strolling around the front yard wielding a welded iron pincer that looks like the kind of thing you use to pick up burning logs. I get out of my car and there is a full-scale reptilian rebellion underway. It seems that in order to make me feel especially welcome, Woody has deposited four or five rattlesnakes on the front lawn.

"I'm just playing with them," he says, smiling like a kid on Christmas morning, flipping them around with his homemade snake stick. I feel the urge to get back in my car. He tells me to throw my precious Wisconsin Badgers Rose Bowl cap at one of them. I do what I'm told. A timber rattler shoots out of the grass like a shot from a rifle. His mouth opens 180 degrees and he sinks his fangs into the bill of my cap. "Now that's nothing but fun," he says. So much for that cap, I'm thinking.

Woody is enjoying himself, maybe even showing off a little. When he announces that it's time to go snake hunting, he suddenly gets very serious.

"I'll take you snake huntin', but we have to have an understanding." I nod my head in assent. "DON'T GET BIT!" He shakes his head violently. "I'M JUST WARNING YOU: DON'T GET BIT. AND IF YOU DO GET BIT, DON'T COME RUNNIN' TO ME."

Woody knows about these things firsthand. After his one-and-only bite a few years ago, he had to be helicoptered to the University of Wisconsin Hospitals.

He rolls up his sleeves. He's got one Popeye-sized forearm, and he tells me it will probably never shrink. For a while there, they didn't think he would make it, but he did. He's one tough old snake hunter. "So I'm tellin' you," he says, "that I know what I'm talkin' about. DON'T GET BIT!"

We get in the truck and drive down the road. He gives me what looks like a big reinforced butterfly net. He is carrying his big snake tongs. The plan is that he will roust out the snakes and I will scoop them up in the net. We go up and down the hills, Woody looking for snake dens, me treading carefully in fear of stepping on a rattlesnake, and Woody keeping up a running monologue.

"I know where they're hiding," he says.

We walk another fifteen minutes through a hayfield. "Isn't it just that way?" he says to no one in particular. "When you don't want a thing, you can always have it. But when you want that thing you just can't find 'em. Don't that just beat all!"

He starts poking under a rock where he swears there's a snake den. Nothing happens. In fact, we haven't seen a snake since his front lawn. He looks at me. "I'll tell you one other good thing about snake huntin'."

What's that?

"It's never crowded," he says, winking in my direction.

We don't catch any rattlesnakes that afternoon. We don't see or hear any. Woody looks lower than whale dung on the floor of the ocean. For my part, what with the big show on the lawn when I arrived, I am feeling satisfied in the snake department. I don't have the heart to tell him that my snake-hunting days are over.

It wasn't a complete failure on my end, I tell him. "How's that?" he asks.

"Well . . . I DIDN'T GET BIT."

When I drove away from his home that spring day in 1995, it was the last time I saw Woody Roberts. He died of cancer at home on February 27, 1997. He was eighty. I never went snake hunting again. I think the sight of all those rattlers on Woody's lawn—combined with the image of his permanently engorged right arm—was enough for me. But he was great fun and living testimony to the saying that, if you're one of the lucky few, you get to keep more than a bit of the boy in the man.

# THE FROGMAN COMETH

## Art Gering and the Astounding
## Amphibian Invasion

It was a foggy, soggy spring night. I was heading home on Highway DL in Merrimac. I had been to the Old Schoolhouse for dinner, where I had fried chicken and a couple of beers. (I might have had three, but absolutely no more, which you'll know is important once you see where this story is headed.) I was doing forty-five, alert as a bird, and just rounding an easy corner when my headlights hit hundreds of bulbous, egg-shaped eyeballs covering the road in front of me. It was a veritable legion of frogs making a forced march up and out of the marshland on my left into the woods across the road.

I hit the brakes and it was like skidding on glare ice. Thump, thump, bump, bump, thump, bump, the rhythm occasionally rocked by the sound of something like a water balloon going squoosh in the night. It was like a scene from one of those cheesy horror movies that occupied the Saturday afternoons of my boyhood. The death toll was considerable. And I don't mind telling you that I felt guilty as hell for having ground so many innocent amphibians into the asphalt.

Honest to God, I avoided that stretch of road—there was an alternate route to the fried chicken—for the rest of the summer.

I wrote a column about the persistent psychological trauma associated with that incident. But, as often happened, one of my readers wrote me a letter that reduced my personal torment to nothingness: compared to the invasion of Oconto, Wisconsin, in July 1952, she informed me, my teeny-weeny frog episode was hardly worth a mention.

When they first hopped out of the stretch of foggy bottom between Pensaukee and Peshtigo harbors along the west side of Green Bay—millions of greenish-gold, black-spotted amphibians behaving like a bunch of sailors on shore leave—some God-fearing folks thought there might be something biblical in the offing.

They took to quoting Exodus 8:3: "And the river shall bring forth frogs abundantly, which shall go up and come into thine house, and into thy bedchamber, and upon thy bed, and into the house of thy servants, and upon thy people, and into thine ovens, and into thy kneadingtroughs."

Of course, it wasn't anything like that at all, just the confluence of light winds, lots of calm water, sunshine, and millions of frog eggs. As a result, for a two-day period in July 1952, Oconto experienced an invasion of frogs like nothing seen before or since.

"It was gross," says Rosemary Rice, recalling the phantasmagorical frog onslaught. She was six years old at the time and still physically squirms at the *smoooosh* of leopard frogs being squashed beneath automobile tires.

The *New Yorker* magazine, in the person of one Eli Waldron, who just happened to grow up in Oconto, arrived to chronicle the event. He wrote:

> The explosions of amphibians beneath the wheels of automobiles at night sounded like rifle fire. People mowing their lawns did so in a storm of flying frog legs and truncated frog bodies. At night you could hear frogs swishing and skittering in the grass and hear them croaking everywhere. . . . There were so many frogs that they piled up on one another, and they seemed so purposeful that a man I know said they had besieged his house one night in what he swore was a highly organized way. He had gone out on his front lawn to have a look around with his flashlight and had been confronted by a million shining little eyes.

I read that during a normal spawning season, about 1 percent of frog eggs—these were *Lithobates pipiens*, or, to the uninitiated, northern leopard frogs—make it to maturity. But in 1952, according to an article in *Discover* magazine, "the water of Green Bay remained at a high level into the summer, and the wind kept whipping water into the adjoining marshes and ponds. Bayside roads crumbled from wetness, and shoreline homes became uninhabitable. But amphibians laid their eggs as usual."

This was a moment made in frog heaven. Three times as many eggs hatched and produced millions of tiny tadpoles that transformed into frogs. There were so many frogs—far too many to share the available mosquitoes, crickets, dragonflies, and moths that usually sustained them in the wetlands—that they fled their usual habitat en masse and headed for Oconto, the county seat, to find food. "Once the frogs arrived," the magazine reported, "they outnumbered the people 35,000 to 1."

This being almost a half century since the great frog offensive, I thought it only fitting to find the world's foremost living authority on the amphibious assault of Oconto. "You'll want Art Gering," says Diane Nichols, president of the local historical society. "He's been here all his life. He used to frog."

The word "frog," I learned then, could be a verb.

"He was a *professional* frogger. And he still lives down by the river."

So I give Arthur Gering, eighty-five, who is to frogs what Michael Jordan was to basketball, a call. I tell Art that I want living history in all its horrifying detail. "Oh yeah, I remember when the frogs came to town that year," says Art, who made his living as a frogger and commercial fisherman for decades. "I frogged all my life. I love frogs. To me, when I see a frog, I see money."

I have never met anyone who knows more about frogs than Art. He was born in May 1915, started frogging with his grandmother when he himself was just a tadpole, and didn't stop frogging until he packed it in at age seventy-seven. He has a monumental—as in someone ought to construct a monument to this man—memory for anything that involves frogs.

"I know frogs," he says. "Why, I probably caught more frogs out of this area than anybody. I'll bet you didn't know that the west side of Green Bay was the best froggin' area in the US. There was that one year when me and my brother Robert caught three ton. We sold them to the local taverns and to that guy down in Oshkosh who had that big wholesale frog business. Of course, we also sold them to people down in Chicago and to that one Chinese restaurant there too. Anyway, that one year we had half of my mother and father's basement filled up with frogs. We had them in kind of a pen down there. They'd like to raise the roof with their singing."

Raise the roof? "It was the vibration," says Art. "Believe you me, *them* were frogs."

Art explains that most of the frogs went to Friday night frog-leg fries at taverns in Oconto and Green Bay, though some went for pickerel or northern bait. Then there was that time when he got three dollars a pound for frogs sold to a biological laboratory in Fort Atkinson. I remind Art that I am looking for more information about the big frog invasion of July 1952. He ignores me.

"There was demand for them frogs back in the forties for pregnancy tests," says Art, who tends to go his own way in conversation. "They used them for some kind of test that detected pregnancy in women. Don't ask me how it worked. My wife had the test one time, and they used the frogs and they presented me with a bill for five dollars. They said the five dollars was for the use of two frogs for the test. I said if they'd told me that first, I could have brought a bagful and saved the five bucks. She turned out to be pregnant too."

Getting back to the reason for my call: "The summer of 1952 was something, all right," says Art. He remembers that the streets near the golf course were just brimming with frogs and the wheel wells of the cars were jammed and the window wells of the houses were stuffed with frogs piled high "like fish filets in a cooler."

"Nothing but frogs as far as the eye could see," he says.

Mr. Waldron, the guy who wrote the piece for the *New Yorker*, said scientists estimated the total local population that July—acknowledging that it was hard to get an exact head count—at 5,030 humans, 175 million frogs, and about 0 mosquitoes.

"The lawns were chock-full, and the curbs and gutters were full too," Art says. "Of course, you had to wash the bottom of your car, what with running over all them frogs and all."

And so, I ask, what exactly happened with all those frogs?

Art pauses for a moment. "You know how long a frog lives? About five or six years if everything's good. Their sex life is, well, you know, pretty much like humans." Art is chuckling now. "They get older and they just do it less. It's like I tell my friends: I could chase bare-naked ladies around the house all day at my age, but if I caught one, I'm not sure what I'd do. Don't get me wrong: I still like girls a lot. I just can't remember why."

People who study this kind of thing say that what happened in Oconto in 1952 still ranks as the "most dramatic population spike of frogs" in US history. Eventually the frogs, whose croaking could be heard all the way down in Green Bay—I got that from Art but it seems like a tall, loud tale to me—returned to the ponds and marshes. Art, who knew frogs up close and personal, died on January 11, 2011, at age ninety-five.

# BIG BRATS, TINY TROPHIES

## Dennis Leffin and the Wondrous White Sausage

Some elements of Wisconsin culture are not to be joked about. These include cheese curds (squooshy or deep fried), smelt, the restorative power
of fried walleye cheeks, Friday night fish fries, raw beat and onion on rye,
brandy, beer, bubblers, the Green Bay Packers, the 1982 Milwaukee
Brewers, septic tanks, muskies and smallmouth bass, euchre, Alice in Dairyland, black-and-white cows, milk regardless of butterfat content, butter,
cheese, deer hunting (including the sight of men driving around small
towns for days with deer carcasses strapped to the front of their pickup
trucks), and a certain cold weather ritual that involves people seated in

shanties on frozen lakes staring at small holes in the ice for hours on end. (The late and lyrical George Vukelich poetically referred to this last pastime as "fishing the hard water.")

None of these things are even remotely funny. And you know what else is really not funny? Anything that has to do with bratwurst. Some people think that it has an incompatible sounding name because how could something with "wurst" in it be considered the best? This is a question that would be asked only by an ignoramus or an interloper from New Jersey—I know because I was that ignoramus once—who cannot pronounce Oconomowoc let alone Lac Courte Oreilles without the *Field Guide to Wisconsin Pronunciation* close at hand.

Only a fool would think that interviewing the Muhammad Ali of competitive bratwurst eating would result in something entertaining.

I imagine this is what it must have been like to discuss cubism with Pablo Picasso. Or the world's most famous equation with Albert Einstein. On a park bench across the street from the Kohler Design Center, I am sitting with Dennis Leffin, perhaps the most accomplished amateur practitioner of his particular art form in the history of Western civilization. He is about to share with me the secret of his superhuman success. What made this man the best who ever ate—no, *devoured*—the great white sausage?

"I never fill up," the champ says. "Even if I eat an enormous amount and sort of fill up, the feeling goes away fast. Then I'm hungry all over again."

At this moment in time, Leffin, fifty-one, has probably won more bratwurst-eating contests than anyone on the face of the Earth. He was to competitive sausage consumption what Babe Ruth was to home runs. A legend in his own time. "I didn't win every bratwurst contest I ever entered, but almost," he says. "And I think even the ones I was runner-up in, I probably could have won."

On the eve of Sheboygan's annual Bratwurst Day celebration, I thought it only fitting to spend a few moments chatting with the champ and, should time permit, taking down a few tips from the master.

◇

Leffin entered his first Sheboygan Bratwurst Day bratwurst-eating contest in 1953, at age nine. Back then there was just a single "open" competition available to all ages and genders, and young Dennis finished second. The winner inhaled 8.5 double brats in twenty minutes while our boy had just started his eighth double at the buzzer. The following year, an eighteen-and-under division was established, and Leffin promptly ate his way to the crown. He won the next five years in a row. If this were Major League Baseball instead of white sausage consumption, he could have made a fortune in free agency.

And, then—as quickly as he reached the top—he retired. Why? "It was the prizes, really," he recalls, looking a trifle pained. "The prizes just weren't worth it. And, of course, there was a lot of talk. It didn't bother me, but it did bother people close to me."

Like any other field of human endeavor, when you are the best, rumors abound.

"Oh, they said all sorts of things," says Dennis, who also won ice-cream-, watermelon-, and—yes—sauerkraut-eating contests in his youth. "They said things like, 'That Leffin boy had to have his stomach pumped,' or 'That Leffin boy didn't eat for a week before the contest,' or 'That Leffin boy was sick for a week after eating all those brats.' None of it was true. I never fasted. I never had my stomach pumped. I never, ever got sick."

Eventually the sting of petty jealousy and crummy prizes faded. In 1983, after a twenty-four-year hiatus, Leffin resurfaced as a brat man. He was runner-up the first year back. (He's confident that he could have won had he not been distracted by counting brat wrappers.) In 1985, he was crowned champ once again.

"That was my last year," says Leffin, an altogether average-sized man, in case you were wondering. "There were personal reasons for quitting. Also, the prizes still weren't much. That last time it was a trophy with a pig on top. I think I gave it to my nephew."

Anyway, I thought it would be a great public service—no, I was not even remotely hoping it would be entertaining, not in that "funny" way—to have the old champion offer a little advice to anyone contemplating a sausage-eating competition. Here, then, are Dennis Leffin's top tips for basic brat inhalation:

1. Eat right up to the time of the contest. Don't fast. Keep those stomach muscles in motion.
2. Don't drink too much during the eat-off. Maybe a swallow here and there but not much more. Liquids will fill you up.
3. Chew but don't *overchew*. Speed is essential. "None of this forty-chews-to-the-bite stuff."
4. Right at the start, unwrap all your brats and let them cool. There's nothing that gets in the way of winning a bratwurst-eating contest like having your tongue broiled at some point by a smoking brat.

And the tip de résistance:

5. Eat your brats and rolls separately, and squeeze the rolls to get the air out. Inflated rolls can occupy potentially valuable stomach space in the crunch.

"And if you win," warns Leffin, wearing the expression that only firsthand experience can provide, "you have to have a tough hide. Because, believe me, the rumors are going to fly."

As the great Ferdinand de Saussure once observed, "Time changes all things; there is no reason why competitive sausage eating should escape this universal law."

In 2004, Johnsonville, the number-one brand of bratwurst, secured the rights to rename the Sheboygan festival Johnsonville Brat Days. A year later, Johnsonville partnered with the International Federation of Competitive Eating (IFOCE), and the amateur sausage-eating event went big time. History was made on August 6, 2005, when Sonya Thomas—aka the Black Widow—downed thirty-five brats in ten minutes. "They say that competitive eating is the battleground against which God and Lucifer battle for men's souls," said IFOCE chairman George Shea. A year later, Takeru Kobayashi, the Roger Federer of professional eating, set another world record by downing fifty-eight brats in ten minutes.

At some point—I wasn't able to find out when or why—the brat-eating competition was ditched. Maybe the fact that it had gone professional turned off the local folks? Too over-the-top for good, God-fearing Wisconsinites? I wouldn't be surprised. In any event, it was resurrected in 2016 and won by a guy named Blaize Koon of Neenah. He returned in August 2018 and won again, inhaling seventeen of the sacred sausages in ten minutes. For his efforts, King Koon received $300, a year's supply of Johnsonville sausage, and the opportunity to donate $500 to the charity of his choice.

Asked what he intended to do with his prize, Koon said that he would "probably buy food with it." You were expecting a down payment on a Rolex?

As for Dennis Leffin, who may well have turned seventy-four in the summer of 2018, he was not a contestant in the 2018 Brat Days main event. I couldn't locate him. It's just as well. His record for brat eating has long since been broken. The game changed dramatically, like baseball after the designated hitter rule and the juiced-up ball. But I'll always remember him as a true champion in a simpler time, when the game was pure.

God bless you, Dennis Leffin, wherever you are and whatever you may be eating.

# DIGNITY IN MOTION

## Jim Herther and the World's Greatest Car Wash

I was having what you would categorize as a less-than-stellar day in September 1997. My son had left home that morning to drive to Marquette High School in Milwaukee and returned two hours later with the car sitting on a flatbed truck. My twelve-year-old daughter had announced that I was not allowed to speak with her friends anymore because "you don't just talk to them, you interrogate them!" And I had just learned that one of my neighbors had been adding his or her trash to the stuff I put on the curb every Monday night in a really cheesy gesture designed to have me—in effect—pay for his garbage pickup.

I was feeling low. So, as I often did when I felt the world closing in on me, I decided to drive from our little farmstead in Ozaukee County along Highway 60 to our cottage on the Wisconsin River in Sauk County. I needed some quiet time to restore my faith in humanity.

That's the day I met Jim Herther.

Once in a great while you meet someone so good or kind that, no matter what the rest of the day has delivered, the simple act of encountering that individual instantly elevates your estimation of the human race.

It might be the young doctor who stitches up your daughter's hand in the emergency room on a Saturday night. Or the mechanic who says, "No, I don't care what that other guy told you, you don't need a new transmission, just a quart of oil." Or the guy from Whitefish Bay who once pulled over on I-94 on a freakishly hot summer day—I was loaded down with vacation gear, one unhappy wife, two kids, and a panting golden retriever—and cheerfully offered to take us to a local auto repair shop and then drove all of us (including the asthmatic dog) ninety miles to our front door.

Jim Herther is one of those day-changers. But he's more than that: he is the undisputed-but-as-yet-unrecognized world's greatest automated car wash attendant. "Doing business right is 85 percent service. So is life," says Herther, thirty-nine, an athletic-looking guy with a blond crew cut and closely clipped sideburns.

Herther manages the Slinger Super Car Wash on Highway 60. It's one of those everything's-up-to-date emporiums with two or three self-service bays where the hard core congregate, alongside one of those fully automated, touchless, brushless tunnels where cars get watered and waxed without benefit of the human hand. Jim believes that even in this automated tunnel of suds, the human touch counts.

When you pull into the Slinger Super Car Wash, here's what happens: You drive up to that cash and credit card machine where you aren't supposed to see another living soul. Then, out of nowhere, Jim slips in between you and the credit card slot. He takes your card—remember this is supposed to be self-service—issues a warm greeting, a brief fishing report regarding Big Cedar Lake, and a weather forecast.

"If it looks like rain," says Jim, "I just tell people to go on home and come back another time. They'll be wasting their money. Sometimes they look a little stunned."

If it's not going to rain, Jim picks up the squeegee from his bucket and, as he continues the conversation, begins moving counterclockwise around your car. He scrubs your windshield. He attacks the bird droppings on the hood. He knocks the helicopters out of your windshield-wiper well. He scrubs the rear of the rearview mirror, front of the rearview mirror, then all the windows on the driver's side.

He heads around the other side of the vehicle and repeats the drill until, finally and with ferocity, he squeegees your grill until the mortal remains of every bug from Hustisford to Hartford have been obliterated.

You cannot get this kind of service in a high-priced, high-touch, detailing car wash anywhere in North America. By the time you are ready to select the wash option from $5 for the big one to $3.50 for a basic scrub, you wouldn't think of taking anything but the top of the line.

But he won't let you.

"I'm an observer of people," he says. "When you pulled into this lane, you intended to just get the $3.50 wash." He can tell I am a value shopper. "Once you met me and we started talking, you started feeling guilty and you decided to take the $4 option. And then once you saw me scrubbing your mirrors and spraying your hubcaps, you couldn't imagine not going with the $5 plan. My advice is to go with your first instinct. The $3.50 wash is all you need today. I don't charge extra for the conversation."

It gets better. You pull into the tunnel and water starts coating your car. And then, faster than you can say Jim Herther, the door behind you descends and Jim and his squeegee are in the tunnel with you and your car and the downpour. He's moving counterclockwise again, scrubbing all manner of crud off your car, hitting your windows again, staying one small step ahead of the water jets.

And when it's all over, and you think you have seen the last of him, you hear a thunderous "THANK YOU" that makes the hair on your neck salute. And there, directly in your rearview mirror, stands Jim Herther waving a moist good-bye with his squeegee.

"It's my job," he says. "I just try and give everybody the same service. It's like when I was a baker and President Reagan came to visit West Bend. I made a cake for the president. Did I make Mr. Reagan a better cake than I would make for any of my other customers? I did not. I treat everybody the same."

And they treat you well in return, eh?

"Well, most of them do. But I had a guy in a big car in here the other day, and he was making small, cutting remarks about the car wash. Finally, I said: 'With all due respect, sir, just because I work in a car wash scrubbing the bugs off your window doesn't mean I am not an intelligent person. So I'll thank you not to cut me down because of the work I do.'"

And then?

"And then," Jim recalls, "he pushed the electric button and rolled his window up. But I felt better for telling him."

When I was doing a semester abroad in England during college, I came across a scene that has stuck with me for decades: a crew digging up a single pothole in a road in the center of Banbury. The tools of their trade were pickaxes and shovels, brooms and big dustpans, and buckets to deposit the refuse in. They worked hard at excavating that hole before they repaired it. They were also dressed in woolen pants and tweed blazers, checked shirts and ties. When it came time for a break from work, they sat on little stools around a bucket of coals that boiled water for a pot of tea. It was a menial task, by most standards, but one thing was obvious: they took pride in their work, and they did it with dignity. Like Jim Herther.

# NEARLY NAKED,
# SEEKING SNOW

## In Wisconsin, That's Amore

I've always been a sucker for romance. I could barely see clearly through the tears to finish the final chapter of *Anna Karenina*. I'm ashamed to admit that I even wept at *Sleepless in Seattle* when Meg Ryan and Tom Hanks—accompanied by that annoying kid—met on Valentine's Day atop the Empire State Building. It was so contrived and I felt so manipulated, and yet I still watch it at least once a year. Maybe it's because as I've aged I've forgotten how it ends.

I felt the same way—only different—about the true-life, not-so-true-love story of the Snow Queen.

Wisconsin men, a macho lot who wear only the finest in camouflage clothing and prefer their bratwurst boiled in beer, have done some really dumb things in the name of love. Or lust. Or a combination thereof. But, in their defense, who hasn't?

Until I became acquainted with the seductive ways of the Snow Queen, I thought the roll call of the Wisconsin Wayward Lovers Hall of Fame would be topped by David Kritzik or Dominic Gugliatto. But first prize should probably be shared by Mr. Z and Mr. M, two amorous gents who lost their hearts—not to mention their pants—to the siren call of Della Dobbe.

You might not remember Mr. Kritzik. He was a multimillionaire industrialist from Milwaukee who, in his late seventies, took up with twin sisters Lynnette Harris and Leigh Ann Conley. The twins, decades younger than their shared boyfriend, had twice appeared together (in the altogether) in *Playboy*. So smitten was Mr. Kritzik with their collective charms that he favored them with cash, furs, and homes worth millions of dollars.

Sadly and misguidedly—and I say this even after the twins sued me in federal court for defiling their good names in print—the US government indicted Lynnette and Leigh Ann, saying they failed to pay taxes on all those nice payments and gifts bestowed by the love-struck Mr. Kritzik. Both were found guilty, but the convictions were later overturned because, in a nutshell, the twins just weren't familiar with the nuances of the federal tax code. Score one for the concept of human kindness and generosity.

Dominic "Nick" Gugliatto was the lovey-dovey lad—also from Milwaukee—who helped convicted murderer Lawrencia Bembenek escape from prison. For his undying love and devotion, Nick was sentenced to twenty-four months in jail and ordered to pay $2,500 in extradition costs. "As God is my witness," Nick swore at sentencing, "if Lawrencia Bembenek came in here now and asked me to help her escape, I would say no!" Ah, Nicky, we are too soon suckered, too late wised up.

However, in retrospect, Mr. Kritzik and Mr. Nick look like two very savvy customers compared with Mr. Z and Mr. M—I don't have the heart to use their full names—of Snow Queen fame.

The Snow Queen, as the cops called her, is actually a lady named Della Dobbe of the little Wisconsin hamlet of Rosholt. According to police reports, on successive winter nights she managed to relieve Mr. Z and Mr. M of their clothing and cash in a most ingenious way.

One cold night in early March, Mr. M was shooting pool at a tavern when Ms. Dobbe arrived. After a few drinks, they decided to step out and visit another tavern. En route to the second establishment in his Ford Bronco, she suggested they park for a bit. That sounded very good to Mr. M.

As kind of an extra special treat, she suggested that Mr. M, soon clad only in his boxers, get out of the truck, gather some snow, bring it back, and let her rub it all over him. (This is what's known in certain parts of northern Wisconsin as "foreplay.") Mr. M, obviously nobody's fool, later told the cops that this suggestion didn't strike him as such a great idea. Nonetheless, he did as he was asked.

"As soon as I stepped out of the vehicle, she was gone," Mr. M told the cops. (Real Wisconsin men always say "vehicle" instead of "car" or "truck," but I have never figured out why.) Along with the Snow Queen went the man's personal possessions, and the miserable Mr. M was left shivering in his shorts.

At the local cop shop, Mr. M was shown a bunch of mug shots. He picked out Ms. Dobbe and, with the sort of conviction that comes with losing your pants while standing in two feet of snow, pointed to her picture and announced, *"I'd never forget that face."*

Things didn't go any smoother for Mr. Z the very next night. He was having a drink at a bar in the city of Wisconsin Rapids—a place appropriately called Critters—when an attractive woman walked in. He bought her a drink. Pretty soon they decided to take off for a casino down the road. Eventually, because this sort of northwoods tavern mating is so intoxicating, they decided to get a motel room.

On the way to the motel, the Snow Queen, being the frugal sort, said they could save a few bucks if they skipped the room and got to know one another in the cab of the truck. Once he was down to his skivvies, Mr. Z was instructed to exit the vehicle and gather snow. "But I don't see any snow nearby," said the befuddled Mr. Z. "Over by the stump, you silly goose," said the Snow Queen. And off into the woods went Mr. Z.

Then, as the criminal complaint quoted our pants-down pal, "away she went." (These guys have a gift for language.) Although the charges against Ms. Dobbe are misdemeanors, each carries a possible $10,000 fine and nine months in jail.

Ordinarily, as a law-abiding citizen who has never lost his pants while scooping snow in his underpants by a tree stump, I would say let the punishment fit the crime. But in this case, assuming these two Einsteins really did take leave of their brains and their britches in the manner alleged, I believe that throwing the book at the Snow Queen would be a miscarriage of justice.

I believe that any woman who can persuade two grain-fed, fully grown (however romantically challenged) Wisconsin guys to get out of a truck on a frigid winter night, clad only in their shorts, and rub snow on themselves or haul it back to a truck in hopes that the Snow Queen will turn them into lovable little snowmen, deserves neither a fine nor a jail cell.

She deserves an Oscar.

As in the best of these bodice-rippers, things ended happily ever after, sort of. The Snow Queen was ordered to repay her victims the money she temporarily borrowed—$1,100—and keep her nose clean for six months. She did both of those things and, in September 1996, the charges were dismissed. As for how things went at home for the guys who parted company with their pants, I can't really say. I didn't have the heart to use their names, and I sure as hell wasn't going to call and ask whether their wives ever forgave them. I prefer to think they did.

# FAREWELL, MY DOBOY

## Kissing Alex P. Dobish Good-Bye

I became managing editor of the *Milwaukee Journal* at the tender age of thirty-six. I had been in the news business for a dozen years at that point, but I was hardly ready to manage a big-city newsroom. There were hundreds of daily decisions involving not just the news and relentless deadlines but legal matters, unions, money, and more. It all reinforced the maxim that working for a daily newspaper was "like being married to a nymphomaniac"—you put one edition to bed and there was another staring you in the face. But I was nothing if not young, hungry, and ambitious. Plus—a recurring theme—the managing editor job paid more.

There were, of course, plenty of people on staff more experienced than me—many of whom probably thought I didn't deserve the job. One of

those was a veteran investigative reporter named Alex Dobish. He was smart and tough and fluent in several languages. He was of Eastern European descent—Russian, I think—and I was told that he had been an interrogator in Europe during World War II. He was also utterly unimpressed with the rosy-cheeked child who was now his boss. Like a lot of reporters, he was good at gathering facts—and maybe the best I ever saw at manipulating news sources—but he was no literary stylist. I took it upon myself to personally edit his bigger stories, and he took to getting even with me.

I learned quickly that there was a price to pay for crossing Dobish.

If he submitted a story for the big Sunday edition late Friday afternoon, I would summon him to my office and tell him why and where the story needed repairing. It wasn't anything personal, just business. Grudgingly, he would agree to fix and refile the story on Saturday morning. Then, because he was terribly courteous, he would cheerily ring me at 6 a.m. to let me know it was done. Then he would hang up.

That was pretty much how it went with me and Dobish. I respected him for his reporting skill and admired him because he was straight out of central casting as a hardball newspaperman and, as a colleague of ours often noted with admiration, he had "the balls of a brass monkey."

Somewhere along the way, he acquired some property on Florida's Gulf Coast. He intended to never wear anything other than shorts and a T-shirt after he retired there, and if anyone cared to contact him—which he was definitely not encouraging—they could find him surf-casting on the beach.

Sadly, Dobish—we cleverly called him the Doboy—died at age sixty-one, not long after he retired. Though I wouldn't have been included if he had personally penned the guest list, I was dutifully dispatched to the funeral as a representative of the newspaper.

It was a cold, gray Saturday in January.

A group of us stood shoulder-to-shoulder in a semicircle in the center of Holy Trinity Russian Orthodox Church on the South Side of Milwaukee. A priest, with eyes like burning coals and a big square beard that major league pitchers favor nowadays, stood at the foot of a coffin. It was a small church and the scent of incense was smothering.

The object of our attention—if not affection—was the poor soul in the box, a recently retired colleague named Alex Dobish, aka the Doboy. He had worked for thirty-one years as a reporter at the *Journal*, broken lots of big stories, dreamed of a retirement spent fishing in Florida, and finally quit. Then he died almost before he had a chance to bait a hook.

Alex was a terrific reporter from the old school, as smooth as silk or rough as sandpaper as the situation dictated. It was our collective belief that the best thing you could do for the education of any summer intern was to seat them next to Dobish. You could learn more about reporting in three months of listening to Alex than in four years of journalism school at Northwestern.

It was a little unsettling to see him lying in state. In any event, at this exact moment inside the little church, a rather imposing Russian Orthodox priest was gesturing for me to step forward, approach the coffin, and kiss Alex Dobish good-bye.

To be candid, I had never imagined smooching the Doboy in life or death, and it certainly wasn't in my thoughts when I knotted my tie that morning. It was not so much about kissing Dobish in particular—he looked quite handsome—but rather the notion of planting my lips on a cold corpse.

I had never been a big fan of funerals—is anybody?—and this one was more exotic than most. The two priests seemed spooky and forbidding with their black kamilavka hats, long boxy beards, flowing black vestments, and strings of strange incantations. What's more, there was no place to sit during the ceremony, the service was interminable, and, throughout, a trio of black-scarved mourners stood in a far corner making the saddest keening sounds I had ever heard. That was saying something, because I had been to my fair share of Roman Catholic funeral Masses that, among other troubling emotions, brought the concept of one's own mortality directly and uncomfortably into play.

(Years later—and I know this is no time for humor so you'll have to excuse me—I thought of the *Seinfeld* episode known to comedy aficionados as "The Conversion." It's the one where George Costanza decides to convert to Latvian Orthodoxy when his girlfriend tells him her parents won't let her date a guy who doesn't belong to their church. George has a chat with the priest overseeing his girlfriend's congregation. When the priest—who looked a lot like the guys who were officiating at the Doboy's funeral—asks George what particular aspect of the religion appeals to him most, George says, "The hats." Of course, I tell that tale reverently.)

Meanwhile, things had gone on awhile when the officiating priest suddenly turned to his left and made eye contact with a woman in black—I believe it was the widow Dobish—and just as subtly nodded toward the coffin. She walked with dignity toward her late husband, leaned over, and kissed his lips. Then, one by one, apparently according to custom, each family member followed suit.

If there were fifty people in that semicircle surrounding the casket—think of the arrangement as the key in front of a basketball hoop with the coffin just inside the foul line—I occupied position twenty-six. I was squarely at the top of the key, five feet from the top of Dobish's thinning pate. Everyone to my right was a relative of one sort or another. I was the first civilian as the semicircle went from right to left.

As the unbroken line of smoochers moved ever closer, I started to wonder: was I expected to walk up and kiss the Doboy bon voyage? I had always been a believer in the when-in-Rome school of etiquette. But it struck me that this Russian Orthodox kissing ritual went well beyond, say, sampling lutefisk and lefse at Christmas Eve dinner with my Norwegian neighbors.

Anyway, by the time my turn arrived, I had convinced myself that I would not be obliged to join in. Only the family members could be expected to kiss the corpse. I was certain these Russian Orthodox folks would be reasonable.

I was wrong. As the last relation on my right kissed the dead man and then trotted back to the spot next to me, the more menacing of the two holy men, the one with the dark eyes with the laser beam focus, looked directly at me. There was no mistake; it was me he wanted. And then he nodded.

Come kiss the Doboy bye-bye, his eyes seemed to say.

I shook my head a couple of times, clearly declining the offer. I didn't make a scene. I also figured that this was like a visitor coming to my own Catholic parish; you were not encouraged to take the sacraments. I knew it would be OK.

It was not OK. The priest tried again. I shook off the sign like a pitcher refusing to throw a fastball when he knew a curve was the right call. The priest was undeterred. He shook his head again. I did not budge. A week seemed to pass. Finally, he fixed me with the most baleful stare. We had passed the stage of polite nodding. His eyes spoke clearly: "I neither know nor care what religious customs you observe, you will step forward right now and kiss Alex Dobish farewell."

And so I did. I had no doubt that this priest could and would outlast me. I walked slowly, respectfully, to the coffin, leaned over—happily found that a strip of delicate paper with Cyrillic lettering lay across the dead man's forehead—and kissed him softly on some mysterious word in Russian script that meant nothing to me, not that it mattered.

One by one, the colleagues to my immediate left followed suit. They, too, looked uncomfortable. But they did their duty, and eventually the semicircle was again unbroken.

I remember nothing else about the ceremony. It could have gone on for two more hours or two more minutes. It wouldn't have mattered to me. I had crossed the threshold.

Later, after the Doboy's mortal remains had been driven away to his final resting place, a group of us stood solemnly inside the vestibule of the little church. We shifted our weight from one foot to the other and stared at the floor, the way men do when something awkward happens and they don't want to discuss it. We were all waiting for some signal, the green light to get out of there. We examined one another's polished shoes, played with the change in our pockets, fumbled for cigarettes, did anything but look at or speak to each other.

Until a guy I will never forget, a rough and ready character named Tom Lubenow from the wilds of Sheboygan, suddenly broke the silence. Speaking to no one specifically but everyone within earshot, he announced, "I figured that if Hannah went ahead and kissed Dobish, I'd kiss him too."

Everybody nodded in agreement. Then we all walked out into the cold and went our separate ways. And, to the best of my recollection, we never again mentioned the day we kissed the Doboy good-bye.

In retrospect, I think I may have underrated Alex Dobish's skill as a writer. After I wrote this chapter, I went back and reread a series he wrote about his own alcoholism called "Corking the Bottle." He had been a closeted alcoholic for a long time and finally decided to open the door. He wrote the series six years before I became his boss—though I never really became his "boss" other than on the organization chart—but we talked about it one day. We sat in my office and I told him that I remembered that series and that it took courage to write and he did so beautifully. He told me that he used to arrive at the office and get an assignment from his editor, then hop in his car and take off for the day. I remembered him telling me that in the trunk of the car was an insulated cooler, filled with ice, surrounding bottles of his drug of choice—white wine. He told me that he would find a convenient parking spot and drink until he was either happy or at least sufficiently self-medicated. That's the way I remember it.

Sometimes your memory is frighteningly good, other times less so. In this case, as my rereading confirmed, I had it right. "I preferred the solitude of the county parks or the hustle and bustle of a crowded parking lot, where few pay attention to a person in a car," Dobish wrote. "My fine choice in wines remained, however. It was good chenin blanc and chablis, cooled to a delighting chill in a special ice chest in the locked car trunk."

There was an explanatory note that ran with every installment of Alex's confessional. It bore the headline "Time to Face, and End, Shame."

He wrote: "When I was admitted recently to the Alcoholism Treatment Unit at Elmbrook Memorial Hospital, I did not plan to write about the experience. I discovered, however, that a great many people, in addition to the alcoholic, are destroyed by this disease unless help is sought. One barrier to getting help is a misguided fear of the social stigma attached to being a recovering alcoholic. Alcoholism is no more a disgrace than diabetes, tuberculosis, or heart disease."

I don't recall what killed Alex. But it's a shame that, after all he had been through and the very public march he made toward recovery, he didn't get more time for fishing.

# PART

**5**

# ANIMALS? YES!!

# PEOPLE? NOT SO MUCH.

Hey, diddle, diddle, the cat and the fiddle, and the elephant jumped over the fence. Photo courtesy of Pat Peckham.

No one ever accused me of being a quick study, but it didn't take long to learn the most valuable lesson not included in the columnist's handbook: if you want a guaranteed response from your audience, write about animals. You can compose the most heartwarming, uplifting story about a heroic human being and be met with deafening silence. But write a story about a dog, turtle, horse, or even a pair of lonely llamas (as I once did) and you'll need a second email server and another phone line to handle the feedback.

In an average week, I'd get fifteen or twenty emails and letters from readers. But write about anything with a beating heart that wasn't human—which I did maybe fifty times out of five hundred or so columns—and I'd get dozens of love letters from readers. Once I wrote a column about having dinner with a man who, six months earlier, had been on death's doorstep after getting caught in a freak storm on Mount Everest. I thought it was one of the most compelling stories I ever had the opportunity to tell. Response? Negligible. Compare that to a column about two amorous emus who went missing from a farm near Mosinee. My email and post office box were overflowing. It was not a fair fight.

Meanwhile, you would think that stories about dogs would get people most fired up, seeing how they are man's best friend and mostly disposed to please. But you would be wrong. Cats are the hands-down biggest draw, even though cats let you know up front that they have little use for you beyond food and something to rub against. It's like the quote from Doc Martin, a veterinarian friend of mine: "Dogs come when they're called; cats take a message and may or may not get back to you."

We once had a calico cat named Little. We called her that because she wasn't as big as the other cat we had at the time. I suppose we could have called her Smaller, but it hadn't occurred to us.

Little used to hide in the house all the time. The only way to locate her was by pressing the handle on an electric can opener and singing, "Here kitty, kitty, kitty." Pause. "Here kitty, kitty, kitty." Eventually the cat would turn up because she thought we were opening a can of cat food. It was a good ploy.

Little was a house cat. On those occasions when she escaped into the great outdoors, she would stay away for a week, return home disgraced and defiled, and sixty days later deliver a pile of kittens. One year she punched out three separate litters. This upset my wife, who ended up in the kitten-placement business.

One winter's day, with the earth covered by two feet of snow, Little bolted out the door while my wife was at work. I knew this would go badly for me when she got home. I needed to find that cat. I hatched a plan. I put on my big, green, waterproof, insulated Farm & Fleet boots. I put on my Pillsbury Doughboy parka. I put on my coveted Russian rabbit-fur hat with extended earflaps that my father-in-law brought back from Moscow. It was sunny outside, so I put on my sunglasses. Even by my suspect sartorial standards, I looked, as my Scottish grandmother used to say, a "wee bit odd."

I got one of those industrial-strength, glow-in-the-dark orange, seventy-five-foot extension cords, plugged it into the garage outlet, and connected the electric can opener with the magical powers. (It was the only foolproof way to get that cat to come out from hiding; she associated the whirr of the can opener with feeding. Otherwise she ignored me.) Then I lifted the garage door, walked out into the yard, high-stepping through the snow, intermittently pressing my can opener, singing, "*Here kitty, kitty, kitty.*" Pause. "*Here kitty, kitty, kitty.*"

My new-ish next-door neighbor was a reclusive widower named Matt Mick. He was wary of me. He had lived in his home for a long time. I was a newcomer to a place that had a natural suspicion of newcomers. On top of that, I had a beard, which he regarded at best as suspicious—why would a man hide part of his face?—and at worst, dangerous. A man with a beard had a fifty-fifty chance of being part of the Manson family.

Mick was standing in his driveway doing some touch-up shoveling when he caught sight of me traipsing through the snow, caressing my electric can opener, dragging a live extension cord, and purring, "*Here kitty, kitty, kitty.*" Pause. "*Here kitty, kitty, kitty.*" I turned to see him staring at me—no, glaring at me. I was embarrassed. Mick was terrified.

I wanted to explain what I was doing. I waved to him as I started my long march in his direction—very slowly—up the little hills and down the little valleys of snowdrift. Mick watched this show for a full thirty seconds, shook his head half in disgust, half in disbelief, then tossed his shovel into a snowbank and retreated inside the safety of his home. I was only halfway there when he disappeared.

Not long after that, Mick sold his house. Not long after that, he died. I never got to explain what I had been doing in the middle of winter dragging an extension cord through the snow singing, *Here kitty, kitty, kitty*. Maybe he thought it was a religious ceremony. In any event, I'm sure he passed on thinking I was not only intentionally tormenting him but an atrocious dresser to boot.

Today, I smile when I tell that story. Back then, I wondered if Mick watching me helped put the man in an early grave. I'll never know. I don't want to know.

And, oh yes: the Little cat returned later that day, waited a few months for the snow to melt, then bolted, never to be seen again.

I know this is supposed to be a book about the two-legged inhabitants of Wisconsin with opposable thumbs. And it is—mostly. But God knows that I would be remiss—plus, it's possible I would sell a few more copies of this masterpiece—if I failed to include a few stories about the four-legged friends who actually made my career, such as it was.

# THE ELEPHANT IN THE ROOM

As my late father taught me, when it comes to horse racing, it's better to be lucky than good. This is doubly true of the news business. You can work really hard to get a story, but there's nothing so gratifying as occasionally catching a break.

One Sunday morning in August 1977—a few years into my stint with the *Milwaukee Journal*—I got lucky. I was living out in the country and driving into metropolitan Sauk City to play tennis. As I passed through the adjacent village of Prairie du Sac, I saw what I took for a hallucination: A very large elephant was cruising up the street in front of me. It pounded down the sidewalk, tore across somebody's front lawn, then turned up the driveway and into the backyard. I had a pretty worthless degree in English but a hyperactive imagination in those days. So I instantly thought of a scene from Ernest Hemingway's *Green Hills of Africa*, only instead of great white hunters tracking a rhino on safari in Tanzania, these were brave

Wisconsin boys standing on the bedliner of a Ford pickup chasing a circus elephant a stone's throw from my favorite tavern on Water Street.

It was an unusual sight. I had never come across an elephant on the loose in Prairie du Sac before—or, for that matter, since. So I joined the chase.

In his most profiteering moment, P. T. Barnum could not have concocted a more astonishing publicity stunt. But this, ladies and gentlemen and children of all ages, was no hoax.

Here is what happened just before midday, a dull and dreary summer afternoon in the little but lyrical village of Prairie du Sac, Wisconsin, when the Carson & Barnes Traveling Circus came to town.

The circus hands, helped by the biggest and strongest of their thirty-one elephants, were hauling up the big top. According to Ted Bowman, the business manager of this traveling road show, the elephants were fully harnessed and in the process of hoisting the poles that support the tent.

Barbara, the very same four-ton pachyderm who made headlines when she bolted from the circus grounds in Fond du Lac a few weeks back, was part of the rigging crew. "She was pulling a pole up but when she almost had it upright, it slid off a bump in the earth and went clattering to the ground with a great commotion," explained Bowman. "The noise must have scared her and, well, she just took off."

"Took off" is a bit of an understatement. For the next two hours, Barbara, all of thirty-six years of age and hobbled by chains connecting her front legs, led the circus animal keepers, local and county cops, the Prairie du Sac and Sauk City Volunteer Fire Departments, and a legion of joyriders on a four-mile jaunt around town.

Sauk-Prairie police sergeant Paul Harman, doing his best imitation of a cop acting like elephants run through here regularly, said: "The elephant first went two blocks east to Water Street and then reversed direction. She went up past the ballpark, past the hospital, and made a beeline straight for the Maplewood Nursing Home on Sycamore Street."

Judy Carr, twenty-four, who is married to the circus elephant trainer, said Barbara never was one to let a mere building deter her. "When she got to the nursing home, she looked into a glass window, saw her reflection, and charged. She busted the glass, stopped, turned to her right and saw another, bigger window, and went straight for that one."

This time, as Norman Kraemer, a resident of Maplewood Nursing Home, tells it, Barbara was not to be denied. She shattered the window of a private room normally inhabited by two elderly women who were thankfully down the hall having lunch and hopped over a three-foot concrete wall. Kraemer said the elephant trucked right on through the ladies' boudoir, through the door, and out into the main hallway bisecting the nursing home.

The accommodating Mr. Kraemer gave me a guided tour of Barbara's route on Sunday afternoon. Once in the hallway, the elephant turned right and headed for the main nurses' station directly down the corridor. For some miraculous reason, the headstrong beast—"No, she's really a sweetheart," insisted Judy Carr—skirted the nurses' station and didn't so much as ruffle a piece of paper. In her wake, Barbara the elephant, who was evidently taller than the ceiling, left behind bent steel ceiling supports, tore out most of the overhead electrical wiring, and brought most of the ceiling tiles tumbling down. The place looked like an elephant had run through it.

Meanwhile, as she headed for the large exit sign to the south, Barbara paused to make a ninety-degree turn into a private room at the end of the hallway where one Harley Hanick, an elderly gentleman with an everlasting devotion to the Green Bay Packers, was watching football on TV.

Harley explained—with the sort of understandable outrage that anyone would feel if the Packers game was rudely interrupted—that the sudden intrusion "was pretty nearly like a tornado, what with all that goddamn racket and all. I went to see just what the hell was going on and walked right over to the door and then this goddamn elephant sticks its head right inside. I slammed that door pretty quick and changed her direction fast enough, you bet!"

Barbara, having had that unfortunate run-in with the hot-headed Harley, now veered to the west, used her trunk to depress the bar across the door leading to the back of the nursing home, and was out in the open air once again. She rumbled along for another mile or so, decided she had seen enough of the local sights, and was captured in a cornfield.

Mrs. Josephine Roos, who is eighty-two, was sitting by the window in her wheelchair, close to where Barbara made her entrance into the nursing home. She is an uncommonly calm human being. She said that the arrival of the elephant had brightened up an otherwise dull Sunday afternoon. "All my life I had to travel to see the circus," deadpanned Josephine, who could have stepped out of a Grant Wood painting, "but today it finally came to me."

Remarkably, not a single hair on a single head was disturbed during the chase and capture. In fact, late Sunday afternoon, there was an air of absolute festivity at Maplewood.

Two elderly gents standing by the reception desk swore up and down—between turns at poking one another in the ribs—that they would never take a drink again.

And a lovely little white-haired wisp of a lady, watching television in a room just off the main corridor, said to me: "This kind of thing is nothing new to us. Have you seen the size of some of the people around this place? Lots of elephants come here to retire."

For his part, Mr. Bowman, the circus manager, took a practical view of the incident: "It's not the kind of publicity we prefer, but if people didn't know we were here before, they sure know it now."

On a Saturday morning in January 2015, I drove from Chicago up to Prairie du Sac to say goodbye to an old friend dying of cancer. We talked about how nice it was to live on our little peninsula jutting out into the Wisconsin River. "It's a little slice of heaven," Don Gattshall told me. "I was lucky to live there. You're lucky to still own your place there." We discussed our old neighbors, our kids, the Green Bay Packers, and the time he removed two rooms of brand new carpeting from my home because there was a mix up and the wrong color was installed. We talked for a couple of hours. He was getting tired and it was time for me to go. I told him what a great friend and neighbor he had been and to keep fighting, although we both knew his time was about up. I was almost out the door when he called my name: "Say, have you been to the Maplewood Nursing Home lately?" No, I said, not lately. He was grinning like a man who had another fifty years in him. "You ought to stop by. The story you wrote about the elephant running through Maplewood is in a big frame right in the hallway. Everybody sees it, and it has your name on it. That was really something, wasn't it?"

# BO KNOWS

We had a hobby farm in Ozaukee County that we sold last year. It had five outbuildings, including two barns. When we moved in, we discovered an old ragamuffin cat living in a cardboard box upstairs in the small white barn. The kids named him Bo. He proceeded to run the place—not just the barn but the entire ten acres, including our house—until the day his kidneys quit. On the spur of the moment, motivated by the fact that I didn't have a column one Friday, I decided to devote the space to old Bo. It took me forty-five minutes to compose. Nothing I wrote before or since has elicited such a response.

Bo had attitude. Our first summer on the farm, the dog next door came loping across the pasture and climbed the porch hoping to introduce himself—Bo promptly bloodied his nose. There was something about him that Bo didn't trust. Turned out he was right.

Bo liked to stay out all night, sleep in all day. He had a good left hook, a cauliflower ear, one blind eye, and the most bowlegged gait since Billy Crystal got off that horse in *City Slickers*. Frankly, Bo didn't have much to recommend him. Worse, he didn't care.

But he grew on you. He had lived upstairs in the old barn for God knows how long, and he considered it his own. Once, when I was moving lawn furniture out of there after the snow melted and he more or less refused to move out of my way, I suggested he might make some sort of contribution if he hoped to stay. He tipped his head, stared at me with utter disdain, and resumed licking his paws.

"Are you as dumb as you seem, Steve?" his eyes said.

My family considered him quite the charmer. They would pick him up and rock him like a baby, then scratch his chewed-up excuse for ears. When they began bringing him inside the house in summer, I was opposed, and loudly so. When I caught him sleeping under the kitchen table one day, I put my considerable foot down.

"That old bag-of-bones barn cat is not moving into this house," I howled. "There's no telling where he was last night. This is a *barn* cat. He stays in the *barn* if he stays at all."

Pretty soon he had vacated the cardboard box in the haymow and taken up residence on a specially prepared lawn chair that had been moved to the back porch. It had a doubled-over, fluffed-up beach towel for a mattress and a parasol to shield Bo's scrawny frame from the sun. Truth to tell, though I railed against him for his arrogance and presumption, I worried a little when late autumn suggested winter.

One day—obviously out of my mind—I stopped at a pet store and invested in one of those insulated, igloo-style pet houses with the heavy-duty plastic flap for coming and going. "There's a nice blue mat that goes with it for another fifteen dollars," said the saleslady.

I was appalled. "Do I strike you as the sort of sap who would spend another fifteen bucks to buy a bed for some shiftless barn cat that has slept on a pile of straw all his sorry life?" I walked around the store feigning interest in bird feeders for ten minutes. Then I forked over the extra fifteen for the mat.

I figured I would get big family points with the igloo. I put it on a bench on the porch and, with Bo lounging nearby, demonstrated how a grateful barn cat that had no visible source of income and relied on the kindness of strangers would go in and out, in and out. Bo took no notice. So I lifted him up and placed him inside. He promptly walked out. He did not walk back in.

"I don't care if you paid two hundred dollars for the whole arrangement," he communicated, quite clearly. "I'm not interested. I'm a cat, not an Eskimo."

A week later he was fast asleep in a laundry basket in the kitchen. A week after that he had moved to the hallway upstairs. Soon he was sawing logs on the end of our bed. I don't remember when he started sleeping between us.

I came to admire his arrogance. He would waltz down for breakfast, and one of the kids would fill his bowl with crunchy cat food. He would look at it disdainfully, then stare at my wife, who was behind the morning paper. He was getting old and his gums were sore and he preferred something softer. In the end, Bo always got his way.

A few weeks later, I noticed that he was struggling to make the leap from the floor to the bed and that his trademark laziness had turned to listlessness. "He's got severe kidney problems," the vet pronounced. "He's in an awful lot of pain. He should be put down."

I was on a business trip to New York when I got the bad news. I don't know what came over me. I couldn't stop thinking about that old cat, how he was the picture of contentment when he slept, how he sauntered down the gravel drive from the barn like he owned the place, how he stared and glared until you got up and substituted smoked salmon for Meow Mix.

When I arrived home no Bo was on the back porch. No Bo asleep on the stairs, refusing to budge. No Bo in the bedroom taking the sun.

After dinner that evening, I strolled out to the barn. I climbed the steps and walked over to the cardboard box that one of the kids had filled with straw when we first encountered the old cat. I stood and stared. Then, alone in that old barn with not a soul in sight—you can bet I made sure of that—I had a good cry.

I must be losing my edge.

# OH, DEER

## The Anna Mae Bauer Story

I didn't have a chance to breathe, let alone brake, when a doe the size of a small horse leaped out of the ditch and flashed in front of my headlights. I struck her squarely in the left flank, heard the sickening thud of metal on flesh and the shattering of glass. I regained control of the car and pulled over on the shoulder of Pioneer Road.

I grabbed a flashlight and started walking along the shoulder back to where either I hit the deer or the deer hit me. On the pavement ten yards ahead of me was the strangest sight: the doe was sitting motionless and upright, its forelegs tucked under its torso, looking like it had just sat down in a bed of grass, alert. I took a few steps closer, half-expecting the doe to stand up and trot into the cornfield. But she didn't move. I figured it was shock.

If you've never hit a deer with your car—Wisconsin racks up about twenty thousand deer-car crashes a year—it is not a pleasant experience. Aside from the damage to vehicles—averaging about $4,000 per incident—it leaves a person with a sickening feeling. As annoying as deer can be when they're chewing the tops off your flowers, they are beautiful, gentle creatures.

I called the Ozaukee County Sheriff's Office that November night, told the dispatcher what had happened, and waited until the deputy got to the scene. Then I left.

My little incident was chump change compared to Anna Mae Bauer's experience.

In her worst waking nightmare, Anna Mae Bauer is heading up Highway 85 when a swarm of whitetail deer suddenly surround her car. Led by a twelve-point buck backed up by dozens of doe and a fawn or two thrown in for effect, the guerrilla deer surround her car, jump her bumper, sideswipe the side-view mirrors, and, finally and most fearfully, dive into the front seat and land in her lap.

It is the venison version of Alfred Hitchcock's *The Birds*.

"You'd have deer on your mind, too, if you hit sixteen," says Anna Mae, an otherwise jolly fifty-eight-year-old who works at Cray Research, sells tombstones on the side, and travels weekends with the Lima Polka Choir. "Sometimes I ask, 'Why me, Lord?' On the other hand, I know with my track record that I'm really lucky to be alive."

Anna Mae is the undisputed and virtually unchallenged Wisconsin state champion in the never-popular Deer-Downed-by-Car competition. Since 1957 or 1958 (she didn't know what lay ahead, so she didn't write down the date of the first kill), she has smacked sixteen deer while driving. Her current car, a Ford Escort, has notched four in the last six years. In 1994, she hit two deer in the same incident.

"The first one this year did $1,400 worth of damage," says Anna Mae, who has a very close relationship with American Family Insurance.

"It was in the shop getting repaired for two weeks. I had them put deer whistles all over the bumper and everything. Nine days after I picked it up, I hit another one."

She has not reached the point of paranoia where she believes deer actually recognize her while she's driving. She thinks the deer problem stems from the fact that she drives about five hundred miles a week back and forth from her home in Durand to her job at Cray Research in Chippewa Falls, and "especially between Durand and Eau Claire, there's lots of deer. Still, it does make a person wonder."

Just so you don't get the wrong impression, Anna Mae Bauer is hardly Bambi's notion of the Terminator, scouring the countryside looking for deer to thump. She's a nice Wisconsin woman with six kids of her own and seventeen grandchildren, has a good job, has no interest in deer hunting, and is kind to her mother. She's just had a thirty-seven-year run of bad luck. And it hurts.

"I cry over each and every one of them. One time I hit a doe and I got out of the car. It was lying there with its big brown eyes open, and I put her head in my lap. I was sobbing. All of a sudden she got up, walked about five feet and fell. Then she did it again. And again! My God, I hope she lived. I was really shook up."

Surprisingly, downing all those deer hasn't been as costly as you might think. American Family classifies it as "an act of God," says Anna Mae, and her run for the record hasn't really affected her rates. But it does affect her lifestyle. "It's gotten to the point where I have to go extra early to work each morning," she says. "I have to factor in enough time to hit a deer, report it, and still get to Chippewa Falls to start my shift."

During the summer and fall of 2019, I tried every trick I knew to locate Anna Mae Bauer: assorted public records, tax records, Durand City Hall, the Pepin County courthouse, and a handful of sheriff's and police departments between Mondovi and Chippewa Falls. I also made about a dozen calls to people with the last name Bauer in Durand and Eau Claire and several spots in between. No dice, as my father used to say.

I feared the worst. Anna Mae had been unceremoniously subtracted from the rolls of the living. It wasn't natural causes that claimed her. Most likely she had met her master after still another—and in this case fatal for both the driver and the driven—collision with a massive buck. She had defied the odds for too long. Rest in peace, Deerslayer.

And then one magical day in May 2019—I won't bore you with the details—I got a call from a very kind lady named Kay Bauer of Menomonee. Yes, she said, she was a distant relative of Anna Mae. ("Anna Mae married a Bauer," she informed me. "She was actually a Martin.") Yes, she said, Anna Mae was very much alive and, to the best of her knowledge, living with her son in Eau Claire. In fact, she had seen her in church not long ago and she looked just fine. And, yes, she said, so very reassuringly, she was pretty sure she could put me in touch with her. And she did.

One morning the phone rang and—be still my heart—it was Anna Mae herself. "I remember you," she said. "You had that column in the *St. Paul Pioneer Press*. There was a nice picture that ran with it." I was momentarily deflected trying to remember how I looked in that picture. Then I cut to the chase. Did you ever hit another deer with your car, Anna Mae?

"How many did I have when we talked?" she asked. Sixteen, I said. "Oh, well, you missed a few," she said, laughing. "I hit three more. I ended up with nineteen. Unless, of course, you count the one that we hit when my granddaughter Stacy was driving my car and I was riding in the passenger seat. That would make twenty. But, you know, even though it was my car, I don't really count it because I wasn't behind the wheel."

She told me how her son Larry had converted his garage into the nicest two-room apartment. She told me that she still travels and sings with the Lima Polka Choir ("You take Bible verses and put them to polka music"). She told me that she got kind of famous for hitting deer and that once when she walked into a police department to report her latest roadkill, the officer who took her statement knew her by reputation. "He knew my name even before I could tell him," she said, a hint of pride in her voice.

She also told me that one day after all the deer killing stopped, a wild turkey ran right out in front of her car and she killed that, too. She didn't think people would believe it so she stopped, plucked some fathers out of the turkey, and put them in her trunk for evidence, along with a little fresh turkey flesh. The problem was that she forgot all about them until one day when her car stunk to high heaven. "Oh, you just wouldn't believe what it smells like to have dead turkey feathers in your trunk," she said. No, I said, I have no firsthand knowledge of that sort of thing. "It's just god-awful," she assured me.

I wondered if American Family Insurance had finally dumped her. "Yes," she said. "They got rid of me not too long ago when I fell asleep at the wheel, slid into a ditch, went through a fence, got tossed out of the car, and ended up in a farm field between rows of vegetables. But I came to my senses pretty quick and the first thing I remember was me lying there and saying, 'Now where the hell is my car?'"

So, that was the last straw, right? "No, I'm still driving," she said. "Why not? I'm with AAA insurance now and I've got the most coverage you've ever heard of."

# PART
## 6

# YOUR LUCKY DAY

Brendan Hannah with Evelyn Ann Fefer, his first-grade teacher. "Brendan knows that only in the dictionary does 'success' come before 'work,'" said the mighty Miss Fefer. Photo by Steve Hannah.

When I think back on it, there were two things that compelled me to write this book. The first was an email that landed in my inbox in the early 2000s, when I was about seven years into writing my "State of Mind" column. It came from a literate friend who was contemplating a new life as a literary agent. He had been reading my column for years in a Madison newspaper and he thought there was a book in it. He said that I seemed taken by a certain kind of person—he called them "self-actualized," a term that sent me immediately to the Google machine—and that my stories about those individuals were clearly the best stuff I produced. Then he provided me a name-by-name roster of the people who fell into that category. I was flattered that he remembered a couple dozen of my hundreds of columns. I resolved to get right to work and write that book. Instead, I promptly took a job as CEO of *The Onion* and obsessed over that for eleven years.

In 2015, a few months from retirement, I read a book called *The Road to Character* by David Brooks. Brooks is the so-called conservative columnist of the *New York Times*, which, as he once said, "was like being the chief rabbi at Mecca." One of the central themes of Brooks's book—these are my words, not his—is that in this digitized age of social media and selfies, a time when genuine human connection is rare and people are building phony "personal brands" and desperately seeking to be "liked" by total strangers, much of the population is in pitiful shape. (It didn't start with social media, mind you, it was only exacerbated by it.) People are needy like never before. Self-absorption has reached epidemic levels, and people live their lives in pursuit of what Brooks called "résumé virtues," that is, prestigious schools, high test scores, then wealth, notoriety, the need to get a leg up on everybody else, and, of course . . . win! These are not new human goals and behaviors; they are just reaching seriously infectious levels today.

Brooks argued that what this morally bankrupt universe really needs is a return to the values that this country was built upon. (His idea of "Make America Great Again" and Donald Trump's are polar opposites.) He called these traits "eulogy virtues," the kind of things you would like people to say you had when they are laying you to rest. These include such antiquated qualities as honesty, integrity, courage, selflessness, self-restraint, modesty, reticence, and, perhaps the most elusive attribute of all, humility.

To illustrate his thesis, Brooks profiles a collection of people who, while by no means saintly—except for Saint Augustine of Hippo—have a certain character shaped by those good qualities. The list included President Dwight D. Eisenhower, General George C. Marshall (responsible for the Marshall Plan that rebuilt Europe after World War II), Dorothy Day (who ran a homeless shelter in New York City and started the Catholic Worker Movement), Frances Perkins (secretary of labor under FDR, architect of many of the New Deal social programs, and the first woman to hold a US cabinet position), the aforementioned Saint Augustine (patron saint of brewers, printers, and theologians), and others. All the people profiled had particular weaknesses to overcome in order to do some good.

While these people of admirable character are all long gone, I was, nonetheless, not shocked to see my name missing from the list. It's not because I'm still among the living or because I didn't orchestrate D-Day and then become president of the United States. No, it's because I am a person who will be chasing "character" until that sunny, seasonally crisp October day when my children delicately dump my ashes off the end of the pier into the Wisconsin River and start me on my journey to the mighty Mississippi. (I'm really hoping that a big gust of wind doesn't rear up and produce a rerun of Donny's service at the end of *The Big Lebowski*.) In any event, I'm looking forward to the trip—but not too soon.

Meanwhile, *The Road to Character* had one other immediate impact on me: It reminded me of that list of people whom my regular reader felt could form the nucleus of a book. I thought about those folks who were, as my late friend Billy Beach used to say, the kind of people you "wanted in your foxhole." They were people who were mainly made up of those "eulogy" virtues. And one other thing about them: Unlike me—or the more famous David Brooks, who admits right up front that he is a "résumé" guy—the people on my list seemed to be of naturally strong character. It was who they were, how they were born and raised. Brooks's people seemed to have the raw material for character formation and a mountain to climb; mine struck me as always having had character,

the way I've always had big ears. Sure, there were things they all over-
came, but by the time I encountered them, they had already arrived.

There was another obvious difference between Mr. Brooks's list and
the one I compiled: His subjects were famous, mine were not. His included a president, a couple of generals, a cabinet officer, and a real,
certified, canonized saint! Mine weren't exactly a butcher, a baker, and a
candlestick maker, and while they were accomplished each in their own
way, they were not household names. They demonstrated their character not on the world's great political and social stages but rather quietly
around home.

They included a mom who became an award-winning poet; a
CIA-trained guerrilla fighter from Laos who served on the city council
in Eau Claire; a Vietnam vet who lost his legs, then tended to the
"enemy" for decades; a husband and wife who ran a dairy farm with
Down syndrome kids who their neighbors suggested should have been
warehoused somewhere; a pint-sized first-grade teacher who had more
personal strength than the great J. J. Watt; a governor's brother who
usually made the news doing something outlandish, then landed somewhere south of rock bottom; and a sweet couple from Iowa County who
taught me the true meaning of that age-old adage, "The joy is in the
journey, not the destination."

It makes complete sense to me that my cast with "character"— as
opposed to just being a cast of characters—were people my late mother
would have loved. They were all smart and kind and funny and terribly
transparent, and each lived what she would have called "unembroi-
dered" lives.

Some I met intentionally, some accidentally. But however I met
them, they shared not only their wit and wisdom but also the precious
example that only genuine people of purpose possess. *They were ordinary
people of extraordinary character.* I think of them—depending on where I
find myself on any given day—often. I need to remember them so they
can guide me.

I saved them for last because they are so special to me. And now
I am going to introduce you to them, one by one. This is your lucky
day.

# POEMS FROM THE EDGE

## Ellen Kort

All night all night
the wind climbs into my bed
slides under my skin
separates flesh from bones
Hung as I am on this wind
I ride it out till morning

**From "Five Ways of Listening
to the Wind," by Ellen Kort**

In 2000 I came across a few paragraphs in a Madison newspaper about a woman named Ellen Kort who had been named Wisconsin's first poet

Living life, like poetry, said Ellen Kort, "is all about going right up to the edge and then . . . jumping." Photo courtesy of Cindy Kort.

laureate by Governor Tommy Thompson. I'm a sucker for all of Wisconsin's official designees—the honeybee (state insect), polka (state dance), trilobite (state fossil), robin (state bird), and, needless to say, Antigo silt loam (our official state soil). I called the poet and we made a date to meet at a coffee shop in Appleton. She was, as the booksellers say, an original first edition.

The other day, Ellen Kort was chosen as Wisconsin's first poet laureate. She is sixty-four, was born in Glenwood City and reared in Menomonie, raised six children she is shamelessly proud of, published seven volumes of poetry, and has a tidy list of literary prizes to her name, including the prestigious Pablo Neruda Literary Prize, named after the Chilean writer who won the Nobel Prize for Literature.

Once, years ago, she was having a rather animated argument with her soon-to-be ex-husband. He waved his finger in her face and announced, imperiously, "What's more, there will be no more of this writing!" To which she replied, calmly, distractedly, the way only a poet would or could, "While you're at it, ask me not to breathe."

Last Tuesday night there was a modest reception in her honor. One daughter arrived to collect her, protested that the poet would likely be late for her own coronation, then whisked her out the door where a big black stretch limousine stocked with fourteen friends and family members sat purring at curbside. The get-together attracted hundreds of admirers from the arts community who, between champagne and hors d'oeuvres, announced they had recently raised $20,000 for a literary fund that Ms. Kort would personally administer.

The poet was genuinely overwhelmed by their generosity. Nonetheless, she managed to find just the right words: "You are all a part of my heart and a part of my story," she told the assemblage, so misty-eyed she could barely see. "We are connected forever."

She "came to poetry late," as she put it, sometime in her thirties. She is unconditionally committed to it. She carries a bucket of glow-in-the-dark chalk in her car, and, for no reason at all except that she just feels like it, she will park in Madison or Milwaukee or Eagle River and compose poetry on the sidewalk or side of a building or anywhere else she pleases.

She conducts poetry workshops for people suffering from AIDS or cancer or other miserable maladies because, she says with certainty, "there is no other time when people need to express themselves so badly." She plans to take poetry to every nook and cranny of this state, and, to prove it, just the other day she accepted an invitation to read her wonderful, carefully crafted words at the grand opening of not the So-and-So Center for Creative Expression but, of all poetic venues, a new Walmart.

"If that isn't grass-roots poetry, I don't know what it is," she says, noting that poetry belongs in the parking lot as much as in the art museum.

She writes beautifully, expressively, viscerally, visually.

In a poem called "What Touches the Skin," she confesses:

> All I wanted was a tiny dove etched on the inside
> Of my left ankle so that when I crossed one leg
> Over the other I could see it and when I stood
> Anklebone to anklebone the small white bird
> Might be carefully caged protected from harm
> Not a symbol of peace exactly but hope

Tommy Thompson, who was governor of Wisconsin for what seemed like forever, eventually took a cabinet job in Washington under President George W. Bush. He phoned Ellen Kort one chilly January day just to see how she was doing. It didn't really sound like that was why he called. He sounded homesick, she said, perhaps even grieving a little. He wondered if the state's First Poet might send him a Wisconsin verse or two, now and then, just "to keep me connected." And she did.

Halfway into writing about Ellen Kort, I decided to conclude this piece with another of her poems, a fanciful piece called "Making a List of People I Could Call in the Middle of the Night." But in the middle of the night I changed my mind. Why? Because this poet is fueled by pure passion and, as she put it, living life, like the best poetry, is all about "going right up to the edge and then . . . jumping."

Anyway, nothing illustrates her passion for poetry like a story she told me—and bear in mind that poets are different from you and me: The youngest of Ellen Kort's six children was a boy, Kris. More than mother and son, they were soul mates, sharing, among other things, a love of language and a special sense of humor. One day, six years ago, because the muse moved her, she wrote a poem called "Instructions to Ashes," in which she described what she would like her family to do when she died—return all borrowed books, have her cremated, and scatter half the poet's ashes in Wisconsin, half in New Zealand.

Kris was troubled by his mother's poem. He couldn't imagine a world without her. At first he refused to read it. Finally he did, though, and it led to a long conversation with his mother about what he would want after his own passing, some distant day down a long, long road. He decided that he didn't want to take up space in a cemetery, and, sort of like his mother, he would like to have his remains scattered half at home, half on a mountain in Colorado.

Three months later, at age twenty-eight, Kris drowned in a sailing accident on Green Bay. His cremation was scheduled for the day before the memorial service. His poet-mother contemplated what was to come and then decided she needed to be there for the cremation.

When the time arrived to return her son to ashes, she asked the funeral director, a kindly man named Tim, if there was any legal reason why she couldn't be the one to actually push the buttons that would commence cremation of her youngest child. No, said Tim, none that he knew of.

"I started him on his first journey," she said. "I think I ought to start him on this next one too." So Tim walked her through the sequence of buttons to push and, at her request, left Ellen alone. She had a twenty-minute heart-to-heart conversation with her youngest child, then pressed the buttons that turned her own flesh and blood to ashes.

While she stood there collecting herself, a fly suddenly landed on her cheek, then moved to her head, then on one arm, then the other. This was no ordinary fly, the poet decided. This insect was inhabited by the spirit of her son Kris.

"You couldn't come back as a majestic, soaring eagle," she remembers saying, out loud, and laughing through the tears as she stood all by her lonesome. "You had to come back as a fly." Wasn't that just like my son's crazy sense of humor? she thought. And she smiled and laughed just a little more before a small wave of sadness washed over her.

Two weeks ago, on what would have been her son's thirty-fourth birthday, the sixty-four-year-old poet laureate and grandmother drove to the Third Dimension tattoo parlor in Appleton and had a fly inscribed on her upper left arm. "It struck me as absolutely the right thing to do," the poet said, tilting her head and searching my eyes. "Don't you think?"

Ellen Kort died at age seventy-nine in April 2015. In 2016, the City of Appleton dedicated a park in her name: Ellen Kort Peace Park. It sits on a two-and-a-half-acre plot of rolling grassland in downtown Appleton, on the banks of the Fox River. She is also part of the inspiration for the city's Sidewalk Poetry Project: When certain squares of sidewalk in the city need to be subtracted, they are replaced by a concrete slab with a poem inscribed in its surface. To date, there are 117 sidewalk slabs of poetry scattered throughout Appleton. Several of them feature poems by Ellen Kort.

I remember thinking, in Kort's company and for years afterward, that I had been in the presence of that rare person who has the unequivocal courage of her convictions. She acted on the truest impulses of her heart and mind, and I'm sure that caused her a certain amount of discomfort. But I imagine that a person like Ellen Kort really has no choice. And, of course, you think about your lesser self in the presence of such an impressive individual.

It made me think about how the only thing I ever really wanted to do was write spy novels, since the first James Bond book I read in junior high school. I plotted and planned to quit every job I ever had and write full time. But unlike Ellen Kort, I pretty much ditched full-time writing—with a few extended return engagements—and opted for making a living, or, as my friends said when I took my first editor's job, "crossed over to the dark side." I spent years running a metropolitan newspaper—hiring and firing, dealing with personnel matters, getting annoyed at union claims, and fretting about budgets at the *Milwaukee Journal*. And, then, after a ten-year interlude in the finance industry, I spent the last eleven years of my professional life as CEO of *The Onion*. Good jobs all, but not what I would have done with my life if I had Ellen Kort's courage. Of course, I wouldn't have made as much money, but I believe I would have been happier. As my late mother used to say, "Too soon old, too late smart." Making money is liberating, and financial security really does help you fall asleep at night, but I am convinced that those things can't provide the kind of joy that comes from deciding to do exactly what you want to do, and then, as Ellen Kort might say, "going right up to the edge and . . . jumping."

# SHORT IN STATURE,
# LONG ON COURAGE

## Joe Bee Xiong

I was having breakfast at the Saint Paul Hotel one morning in April 1996 and reading the Minneapolis *Star Tribune* when I came across a brief: Joe Bee Xiong, a refugee from a mountain village in the highlands of Laos, had been elected to the city council of Eau Claire, Wisconsin, thus becoming the first Laotian to be elected to public office in the United States. It was two plain paragraphs that made me think how very small and interconnected this world truly is.

I knew a little bit about the Hmong and their migration to the United States. When these proud people started arriving in Wisconsin after the Vietnam War—they had been our allies, trained as guerrilla fighters by the

"I think America is a country of opportunity," said Joe Bee. "Anything you want to be, you can be." Photo courtesy of Dan Reiland.

CIA to fight the communists—I had written a series of articles aimed at introducing them to their new neighbors in Milwaukee, Madison, Wausau, and Eau Claire.

As I drove east from St. Paul toward home, I wondered if Joe Bee Xiong wasn't very different indeed from his colleagues on the city council. I suspected that he had traveled a very dangerous path from his village in the Laotian highlands to a small city in western Wisconsin. So I called Joe and asked to meet him. "Of course," he said. "How about 5 p.m.?"

We sat in a back booth at McDonald's, the quintessential American meeting place. I congratulated him on his election. He was the first Laotian immigrant to be elected to public office in the United States, but frankly, I had zero interest in the political issues in Eau Claire. Instead, I asked him straight off if he had been trained by the CIA back in Laos. Yes, he said. What weapon had he carried? An M16, he said. And how old were you when you first killed a man in combat? I was eleven or twelve, he said.

Was there one day in his life as a boy soldier that stood out among all others? "Yes," he answered, without hesitation. "It was the day of the big fight."

It was eight thirty on a damp, dreary morning in April 1978. Joe Bee Xiong and a handful of his CIA-trained colleagues were making their way through the jungle at the base of a mountain in Laos. When the North Vietnamese opened fire, all hell broke loose. The explosion from the enemy AK-47s was deafening. Joe Bee shouted for the other Hmong boys to hit the ground, but not before the air was filled with falling leaves, shredded bamboo shoots, and sliced tree branches. It was as if the canopy covering the jungle had suddenly collapsed.

Two of Joe Bee's good friends died right away. His best friend, Kue, was hit in the thigh and side but was still alive. The first round tore through the top of Kue's leg, exposing a mass of blood and muscle. The second struck Kue in the side but did not exit. It was the side wound that worried Joe Bee most of all.

When the shooting subsided, Joe Bee crawled to where Kue lay wounded on the jungle floor. He slung his own M16 over one shoulder. Then, gently, Joe lifted Kue onto his back.

"It was very heavy with the guns and Kue, and I was shaky," he tells me eighteen years later at McDonald's on Water Street, about eight thousand miles from the scene of battle. The politician Joe Bee, maybe five feet tall and built like a block of granite, wears a gray herringbone sport coat with an American flag prominently pinned to his lapel. We share a pile of cold french fries. There is a kindness, bordering on softness, in his eyes. But also an unmistakable intensity.

"I was able to carry him maybe only 150 yards," said Joe Bee, a hint of guilt in his voice. "He was too heavy. So I carried him behind a rock, sat him up, and put the gun in his hands."

From the front of McDonald's, a salt-and-pepper-haired man shouts as he spots us: "Congratulations, Joe Bee!"

"Thank you," Joe says.

"So Kue is now leaning against the rock," Joe Bee says. "And I say to him, 'Old friend, I do not know if you will survive. I only know I cannot carry you any farther. I will go get help and come back for you.'"

Joe had entered the CIA's employ at age twelve. He volunteered to take his father's place in the secret army, so his father could return home to his mother. Joe became one of the Hmong boys enlisted to beat back communism. It was a losing proposition. In 1975, the Americans withdrew, leaving the Hmong to face the North Vietnamese alone.

"There are three types of people in Laos," Joe tells me. "The first group flees the country. The second group surrenders and accepts the communist system. I am part of the third group, the group that fights back and will not accept their ways."

The booth next door suddenly fills with six kids from the University of Wisconsin–Eau Claire. They are alternately swooning about spring break in Florida and moaning about how many credits it takes to graduate. They don't know Joe Bee from Ronald McDonald.

"After the Americans left," Joe Bee resumes, "those of us in the third group fled our villages and lived in the jungle. Like the fox. Like the tiger. We have no choice. There is no future. We fight to save our families, to protect our villages. We killed many. We poisoned their water. We were very mad."

A man walks over and extends his hand toward Joe Bee. He apologizes for interrupting but, he explains, he just has to offer his congratulations. "I will do my best," says Joe Bee.

"You'll do a good . . . no, a great job," says the admirer.

After he left Kue next to the rock, Joe Bee made his way back to camp through the jungle. He gathered twelve armed men, and they returned to get Kue. It was raining when they found him. "Kue was where I had left him, sitting up with a gun in his hands," recalls Joe Bee. "But he was already dead. I carried him as far as I could. But with the guns, he was just too heavy."

Joe Bee pokes at a cold french fry. He is looking down at the table-top. After all these years, the buried pain from that day rises readily to the surface. His jaw clenches. "During the fight that day, I was never scared," he remembers. He looks me straight in the eye. Whatever else went wrong that day, he wants me to know that he was not afraid.

He says, "I am always the one who calls out to the others to continue fighting. But maybe I call too loud. In my growing up I always have the behavior of leadership. But later, long after the fight, after Kue has died, I am very shaky. I am also very mad and cannot sleep."

Not too long after that "big fight," Joe Bee leads his mother and father, five brothers and one sister, and three thousand other Hmong refugees on a three-month trek across the mountains to the Mekong River and into Thailand. They spend six months in a refugee camp. After that, he immigrates to Philadelphia—which he doesn't like much—then eventually to a lyrical city called Eau Claire in a lyrical place called Wisconsin. He doesn't speak a word of English. But he works hard and eventually graduates from Memorial High School, Chippewa Valley Technical School, and Mount Senario College in Ladysmith, with a bachelor's degree in computer science.

And then just the other day, Joe Bee Xiong, a refugee and wise old man of thirty-four, a father, homeowner, and landlord who pays taxes on sixteen rental properties, was elected to public office in Eau Claire. A loose translation of the word "Hmong," Joe tells me, is "free people."

He feels free for the first time in his life—and very lucky. "I think America is a great country," Joe declares. "It is a country of opportunity. Anything you want to be, you can be."

Now Joe Bee, who learned to fight for his life as a boy, will take his place in the great game of American politics. He will represent his community, family, friends, and neighbors. It is a big, new, public responsibility. "People are concerned about potholes," he says. "Also garbage pickup."

I think about how far Joe Bee has traveled and what it took to get here, and, for whatever reason, I find this talk of potholes and trash collection bordering on the comical. But I don't say that, of course, because he is deadly serious. Instead I ask Joe Bee if he is afraid of his new responsibility.

"No, I am not scared," he replies. "I have seen much life and death. I know what it is to be scared. The city council of Eau Claire is a big job, but, you know, I cannot say that I am scared."

I visited Joe Bee at a ribbon-cutting ceremony in Eau Claire a year after we first met. He was a full-fledged American politician—minus the cynicism. He wanted to serve all the citizens of his adopted home. He was also eager to help the Hmong community take advantage of what America had to offer, but, at the same time, hold fast to their native culture.

When we met that second time—I was shooting a TV piece about his life—it was just after election day. He made a point of telling me that he had just voted. He had become an American citizen in 1986, and he thought that exercising the right to vote was not just a privilege of democracy; it was a solemn obligation.

"Anyone in America who does not vote," he told me, "has no right to complain."

Joe Bee Xiong died unexpectedly of a heart attack on March 31, 2007. He was forty-five. He died in Laos, where he had taken his mother for a visit to the village they fled in the late 1970s. He left behind a wife and eight children. His body was shipped back to Eau Claire. His funeral, a traditional Hmong affair, lasted three days, and an estimated three thousand people paid their respects. Today, the street that he lived on in the place where he built a new life—thousands of miles away from the highlands of Laos, where he struggled to save his friend Kue on the day of the "big fight"—has been officially renamed Xiong Boulevard.

# MAKING BEAUTIFUL MUSIC

## Steve O'Donnell

It was two days before Thanksgiving. I was standing inside Steve O'Donnell's shop, situated in a gentle valley in the Driftless Area of southwestern Wisconsin. Directly in front of me was some sort of contraption—wood and hinges and a collection of gauges—that I could not identify. "What you're looking at is the fuselage of an airplane," said Steve. "Those two big things over there that look like wings are just that—wings." He unrolled a blueprint and spread it on the table. "It's a 1937 Pietenpol. The fuselage is made from a supple kind of mahogany. I'm building it this winter, but next spring I'll be flying it over the hills out there. I love to fly."

I park my car at the end of the winding drive overlooking the snow-covered peaks and pockets of the Kickapoo Valley. Then I walk, stumble, slip, and finally slide through the snow down the stairs to the front door of Steve O'Donnell's shop. It is an auspicious arrival.

I walk in, unannounced, sugar-coated with snow. Steve is perched atop a stool, caressing a wooden flute in his long, lithe artist's fingers. He has shoulder-length brown hair going to gray, gold wire-rims, and a peaceful, easy smile. Something about him reminds me of John Lennon.

"Hello," he says. "Welcome."

To my left is what looks to be one-half of a canoe sawed in two, standing on its wide end, with glass doors hinged across the front. "I originally made it to canoe in," he says, frowning. "But it was tippy as hell. Now it's a cabinet."

Under the worktable there is a whole box of dark, rich-looking cedar flutes, a dozen or more. "I make flutes," he says, examining one the way a pediatrician might inspect a small, delicate child. "I made five hundred or so before I got it right."

He turns the flute again. "It's in my blood to make things."

Steve O'Donnell, forty-eight, came to the Kickapoo Valley twenty-one years ago. Raised in the suburbs of Chicago, he taught school after college. Later he did time as principal of a parochial school in Plain, Wisconsin, until he had had enough. He had already figured out that what he really wanted to do was live in the Kickapoo Valley and make things from wood.

So he bought seventy-five acres of land. First he lived in a cabin, then a house. He worked in a cabinet shop and also made insulated shutters. Along the way, he married a lady named Doreen and produced three handsome—and terribly polite—children.

Eventually, he left the shop and started building his own cabinets, cradles, chairs, and chests. Soon, he won prizes at art fairs across the Midwest and was showing his work at the prestigious Philadelphia Museum of Art Craft Show.

"I'll show you," he says.

Beneath the shop there is a storage room stocked with wood and, along one wall, a collection of oddly shaped objects wrapped in the kind of tufted blankets that movers use to protect furniture. He removes the coverings to reveal three extraordinary wooden chairs—a walnut desk chair and two rockers—one made from light tiger maple with what looks like flames etched in the wood, the other burgundy-colored bubinga, a dark, dense wood from central Africa.

They are exquisite not just to look at but to sit in as well. They are also not for the faint of pocketbook, which seems fair enough since they are not only chairs but also works of art. The walnut chair sells for $3,800, the bubinga rockers for $4,000. You get what you pay for, I figure.

"When I was eleven, I remember staring at a pile of lumber in my backyard and thinking, 'I'd really like to build a big, beautiful boat,'" the artist says. He smiles and points at his creations. "Well, they're not exactly boats, but I think they're beautiful."

A few years ago, Steve O'Donnell had a dream. When he woke up, he remembers, "I needed to make a flute." Not just any flute, mind you, but the flute of his dreams, a beautiful wooden piece that would somehow cross a Native American instrument with a classical European woodwind. The Indian influence would give the instrument a rich, haunting sound, while the European notes would add precision and clarity.

A tall order presumably, and likely the reason that he made hundreds before he got it right. Today his Watershed flute is made in bubinga, cedar, and tiger maple. Recently, the flute was the centerpiece in a recording by the London Philharmonic. It's also prominently featured on the soundtrack of the feature-length film *Alaska* and the Hallmark Hall of Fame production of *Hiawatha*.

Without fanfare, he begins to serenade me. The sound slips from the flute and spirals up to the ceiling. We are interrupted by a knock at the door. In walks a man with his wife, daughter, and grandchild. His name is Russ Holte, a retired teacher who taught for thirty-three years in nearby Westby. He wants to buy a flute.

Steve resumes playing. The shop is suddenly filled with the most soothing of sounds, a strong, warm, resonant tone that—at least in this quiet, gentle valley on a snowy November evening in the woods of western Wisconsin—convinces me that all is right with the world.

Russ Holte says that he, too, has dreamt of playing the flute. Steve O'Donnell, the picture of calm and contentment in his shop this night, says that he will do his part to make the dream come true.

I linger—this is such a beautiful, peaceful place out in the middle of nowhere—and we talk some more about that antique Pietenpol plane that he is building. Next summer, he and his oldest boy, Danny, will thread their way over and around the Kickapoo hills and valleys. Danny, his father says, loves old airplanes.

"He can identify them just by the sound of their engines," the humble man brags about his son. "At the EAA [Experimental Aircraft Association] show in Oshkosh last summer, Danny said he could hear a very specific plane coming our way. There were a bunch of old flyboys nearby and they just laughed. Then the plane came into view and it was just the way he called it."

It was getting late and still snowing, and I had a two-hour drive ahead of me. I packed up my things. We shook hands. He had one more thing to tell me.

"Almost every day I get this sublime feeling," says Steve O'Donnell. "My wife is very beautiful, my children are learning to do *so* much, and I am making things from beautiful wood. It's exactly what I set out to do with my life. And yet, it has exceeded my expectations."

Two months later, Steve traveled to New Mexico with a friend from Viroqua, Bill Essenburg. They had purchased an old Aeronca airplane. Steve and Bill intended to fly the plane back to Wisconsin. Just before takeoff, they posed for a picture standing next to the aircraft. Not long afterward, the plane crashed near Moriarty, New Mexico, after a refueling stop. Steve and Bill were killed. The camera with Steve's pictures was recovered intact.

It was a shock to everyone who knew Steve. His ashes were returned to the Kickapoo Valley, and a potter friend donated an urn to hold them. At the standing-room-only memorial service at a Lutheran church outside Viroqua, Steve's older brother spoke: "I took the conventional route," said Joe O'Donnell. "I wear the tie. He went his own way. But he always wanted to learn, and he was always learning."

"Action was Steve," another friend added. "He put his energy and passion into everything he did." His flutes and furniture "were meant for movement. People were intended to move through them and with them."

I admired Steve O'Donnell and I relished my time with him. He was kind, gifted, calming, and fiercely independent. He was one of those rare individuals who, the moment you enter their field of presence, slow your heart rate in a healthy, measured way.

Unexpectedly, ten days after we spent that afternoon and evening in his studio, the UPS guy dropped off a package at my home. Inside was a handwritten note from Steve. "Thanks for the column," he wrote. He mentioned that he sold some flutes as a result.

The box was packed with Styrofoam peanuts. In the middle was a jar of the O'Donnell family's home-tapped maple syrup. We had pancakes that weekend.

# A NATURALIST'S JOURNEY

## Ken Lange

I made my first trip to Devil's Lake State Park on a sunny Saturday in October 1971. I drove in past a wide open prairie that looked like a snapshot from a travel guide to Montana, up a hill lined with quartzite blocks, past the old Civilian Conservation Corps campground where men found work and self-respect during the Great Depression, and finally down through the pine forests that—out of nowhere—revealed a placid lake in the middle of a deep gorge. True, I was a guy who hadn't seen much of my own country's natural beauty before I came to Devil's Lake that day, but it was surely the most breathtaking sight I had ever seen. Now, almost a half century later, that ten-thousand-acre jewel is no less magical to me. I still hike there in early morning during summer and fall, cross-country ski its trails in winter.

"Not until I returned home," said Ken Lange, "did the outdoors weave its magic in me." Photo courtesy of R. Smith.

It is probably my single favorite place in Wisconsin, and not just because it's a stone's throw from home—though that helps.

Ken Lange was the resident naturalist at Devil's Lake for thirty years, and he knew everything there was to know about this natural master-piece. I encountered him on and off over the years but didn't know him well. Then, early one summer morning, I was hiking the Steinke Basin when I came across Ken and his wife, Esther, binoculars at the ready, resting on a bench. "One of these days," I told him, "I'd love to walk this trail with you and learn what's really going on here." "Anytime," he said. "These days I make up my own schedule." A month later we took a hike together.

The opening line of one chapter in Ken Lange's latest book, *A Naturalist's Journey*, reads, "Robert Louis Stevenson once said that some landscapes cry out for a story." I would twist that statement just a little: I would say the landscape of some lives is worth a story.

Certainly the landscape of Ken Lange's life makes interesting reading.

I hadn't seen or talked to Ken in years, until, one recent summer morning, we crossed paths on the trails of the Steinke Basin at Devil's Lake. He was with his wife, Esther, and I was walking the trail with my daughter, Jamie.

He asked if I had read his latest book. I said I hadn't. He said there was a chapter about the Steinke Basin—my flat-out favorite part of this ten-thousand-acre paradise—in his book. He thought I would enjoy it. I bought the book later that day and read it over the next few weeks. I was surprised to find that it was more than a naturalist's guide. It was a fragment of Ken Lange's autobiography.

In some ways, Ken was an unlikely candidate to become the person who knows more about Devil's Lake—it's a park that attracts in excess of three million visitors a year, about the same as Glacier National Park in Montana—than any living soul.

He was born and raised on the west side of Milwaukee, not exactly a breeding ground for students of natural history. He went to Washington High School, where he graduated in the same class as three guys who made big marks: Bud Selig, who became commissioner of Major League Baseball; Herb Kohl, who became US Senator Herbert Kohl; and a man named Matthias Koehl, who succeeded the notorious George Lincoln Rockwell as head of the American Nazi Party.

Ken graduated from the University of Wisconsin–Madison and then earned a graduate degree in biology at the University of Arizona. From there he went to Washington to work for the Smithsonian Institution. His first assignment was as part of a team studying the plants and animals of Madagascar, in the Indian Ocean. He spent a year studying mammals all over the island nation.

But he was restless in the world of research. He wanted to become a naturalist. So when he heard there was an opening at Devil's Lake back home in Wisconsin, he applied for the job.

On this morning September morning, we meet at a parking lot off Highway DL and set off on the Steinke Basin loop. "August Derleth [a well-known writer who grew up in nearby Sauk City] once said that certain places have a personal geography," Ken told me. "That's true for me here."

He started pointing this way and that: "That's Willow Ridge over there. That row of pines in the distance is what I call Marching Pine Ridge. I'll show you a place I call the High Meadow. And later I'll take you to what I always refer to as the Wedding Place, a spot on the big loop in the southeast corner of the basin where Esther and I were married."

He spent a good deal of time talking about the most recent glacier that covered this place twelve thousand years ago and shaped everything we encountered. He told me about extinct glacial lakes that once existed here, "like beads on a necklace, scattered along the edge of the glacier," and the terminal and recessional moraines. He talked about the variety of wildlife that inhabits the park—whitetail deer, fox, mink, nesting hawks, rattlesnakes, and all manner of songbirds. He told me about the ancient rivers that were rerouted during the ice age, and pointed out a rock that was estimated to be 520 million years old. "Nature," he said, "is one inexorably altering force."

In a place where three million people come to visit each year, to swim and fish and camp and climb rocks, the Steinke Basin is an oasis. "It's my favorite place in the park," he said. "It's away from the crowds, away from the noise," he said. "I always find it incredibly peaceful and quiet. It's a place to think."

We stopped and stood on a sturdy wooden bridge over a creek. "I've seen this bed swollen with roaring water in spring, and at other times so dry it smelled like a hayfield."

We stopped at the Wedding Place: "It's like Henry David Thoreau said: a simple road can elicit many thoughts that you never knew you had. It's true of this place for me."

When he first arrived at Devil's Lake, Ken was mainly absorbed by the natural history of things. Through the years, however, he became more and more interested in the intersection of human history and natural events. Not so much the history of ancient civilizations that once occupied this piece of earth but the people Ken Lange had come to know—directly and indirectly. As we walked up and down the Steinke trail, he talked about a farmer named Archie Johnson; the Steinke family that lived here until the mid-1970s and never had electricity; and, most poignantly, a bachelor farmer named Fred Marquardt, who years ago scratched out a living from this land where eager backpackers now flock to get away from civilization.

Fred Marquardt, said Ken, sent his hired man home for lunch one day in 1935, then shot himself in the head. "He couldn't stand the pain," Ken said. "I think he died of pure loneliness."

Ken led the way through tall grass and brambles until we reached what remained of Fred Marquardt's home: concrete sections of the old machine shed; a depression where the lonesome farmer's house once stood; cultivated plants like roses and peonies that still grew seventy years after Fred Marquardt took his life. "Getting to know about the people who once lived here has added depth," he explained, standing alongside the place where Marquardt's home once stood.

This is the kind of place that Henry David Thoreau referred to, a road that elicits thoughts that a person never knew were there. In Ken's *Naturalist's Journey* there is a moving passage about Fred Marquardt and, not surprisingly, about a younger Ken Lange. Ken noted that in his own youth, far from home, he, too, was despondent and lonely.

He wrote, "I found myself adrift and wondering where I was heading. Not until I returned to my home and Devil's Lake State Park did I truly achieve direction and meaning in my life, for not until then did the outdoors weave its magic in me."

So here is the paradox: the same landscape that Ken Lange associates with peacefulness and natural beauty had, for the farmer who toiled here, become a source of despair and desperation. "And I wonder, if our roles had been reversed," said Ken, "and I had been the bachelor farmer, what then? Thinking of my earlier years, the years when I was lonely and adrift, I empathize with Fred Marquardt and have come to grieve for him."

I had known Ken only casually through the years. He conducted thousands of tours of Devil's Lake, explaining the geography, geology, topography, general science, and history of this beautiful place. Like everyone else you come across in your life, you form a picture of them in your mind. Maybe you even think you know them. In my mind he was a disciplined scientist, a man who could recognize and recite the history of every inch of Devil's Lake. And then one day you take a long walk in the woods with him, and you find out there is so much more to his story than you ever imagined.

"An early morning walk is a blessing for the whole day."
HENRY DAVID THOREAU

I spoke with Ken Lange not long ago. He and Esther have moved to an apartment in Baraboo. He is eighty-four years old, and he says his health is good. Recently he and Esther were honored by the city fathers of Baraboo for their significant contribution to the community. I asked him if it was like being inducted into the Major League Baseball Hall of Fame. He laughed. "It was a humbling experience," he said. "You'll have to ask someone else what it means."

He told me that he had written two books in the last few years. One was called *Song of Place* and the other *Pet Crow and Ice Dragons*. I wondered about the title of that second one. "Well, I once had a pet crow, and ice dragons are glaciers." That's all he said. It was apparent that if I wanted to learn anything more, I would have to buy the books. And I did.

"And, yes, I still walk Steinke Basin regularly," he added. "Esther and I did the big loop just last week."

# RUNNING FOR HELP

## Sue Birschbach and Barb Klinner

Most of what you do when you tell a person's story in print is capture a fleeting moment in time. If you think of each life as a biography, what you are recording is a single scene—or, with luck, maybe a chapter—from a much longer story. Seldom in the news business do you go beyond a single episode in someone's life. And even less often do you get to play a role, however minor, in the story you are telling. On those rare occasions, it can make you feel like what you are doing actually matters.

"I thought about Sue Birschbach (*above*) and her courage all through that race," said Barb Klinner. "The whole sequence of events changed my life." Photos courtesy of Barb Klinner and Gordon Birschbach.

Back in December 1996, I wrote a column about a young woman named Susan Birschbach. She was smart, pretty, charming, and—despite her circumstances at the time—very, very funny. She had everything going for her except one persistent problem: She was seventeen years old and had acute lymphocytic leukemia. She was first diagnosed at age ten. Seven years later she was still fighting for her life.

Nothing could smother her spirit, and absolutely nothing could stifle her sense of humor. When she found out that one of her brothers, Kevin, was a good match for a bone-marrow transplant, she sighed and said there was a definite trade-off in the offing: "Kevin is a terrible speller." She had just received a scholarship to Purdue University, where she was planning to enroll the following fall. "What I'm worried about is that I'll never be able to spell again."

Aside from all her other gifts, Sue was the quintessential Green Bay Packers fan. Once, when she was recovering from chemotherapy and the great Packer Reggie White was out with an injury, she was watching Green Bay play Tampa Bay on television. The cameras panned the stadium and came to rest on a sign in the crowd: "Bring Health to Reggie and Sue in Milwaukee Too." That made her squeal with delight.

"That was it for me," she told me at the time. "You have to understand that to be on TV on the same banner with Reggie White is amazing . . . just amazing."

I had a friend named Vernon Biever who had been the official photographer of the Packers since the ice age. I asked if he could get a couple of pictures personally autographed for Sue Birschbach. "Let's get Reggie White," I said, "and throw in Brett Favre for good measure." They arrived a week later. I took them to Sue and she was over the moon. Beneath Reggie White's autograph he had written: "1 Corinthians 13:7." Sue got it immediately. "Good choice," she said. I went home and dug out the Bible and looked it up.

"Love bears all things, hopes all things, endures all things. Love never fails."

But cancer treatment sometimes does fail. Sue Birschbach died a short time later. Her father, Gordy, said the marrow transplant had gone well but the chemotherapy and radiation had been too taxing for her liver.

At the funeral, six brothers carried their sister's coffin from Saint Cecilia's Church in Thiensville, and each wore one of Sue's many baseball caps. She started wearing them when her hair began falling out. "Sue would have loved it," her father said.

After she died, they found a will—labeled "William"—on her hard drive. "I realize that the process of grieving is hard enough without having to guess what my wishes really are," she wrote. "I remain optimistic that no one will read this until I am old and gray, but at the same time I will be realistic in order to help you, my family. I want you to know that I remain optimistic and wrote this . . . not because I lost hope."

With that she listed her prize possessions—everything from stuffed animals to, yes, her autographed pictures of Brett Favre and Reggie White—and carefully directed the distribution. She passed on a $17,500 scholarship award for academic achievement to a niece named Amy. "As a reminder that any dream can be reached if you strive hard enough," she wrote.

They say that when people are dying, even when they shut their eyes for the last time and drift away, they are often acutely aware of what's going on around them. When Sue shut her eyes at Childrens Hospital of Wisconsin in Wauwatosa, not long before she passed, a mountain of a man quietly appeared in the isolation unit at her bedside. He stood next to her, rested his big hand on her pillow, and prayed.

It was Reggie White. Sue's father, Gordy, was convinced that Sue knew he was there.

About two hundred miles to the northwest, a woman named Barbara Klinner read my columns about Sue Birschbach. There was a reason they struck a chord: she had been a nurse on the cancer unit at University of Wisconsin Hospitals in Madison and had witnessed the heartbreak of people—particularly young people—dying of cancer. She clipped the columns out of her local newspaper and tucked them away. She wanted to do something to honor the memory of Sue Birschbach, whom she had never known personally but felt as if she had.

The clipping stayed in a drawer for about two years. One day I got a letter from Barb Klinner saying that she wanted to do something for the Birschbach family. That summer, she had decided, she would run the San Diego Marathon, all 26.2 hot and humid miles of it, in honor of Sue Birschbach. She would be part of the Leukemia Society of America's Team in Training, and, through pledges from friends and family, she would raise money for cancer research.

She wrote to Sue Birschbach's parents, Gordy and Barbara, and told them what she intended to do. They blessed her good heart. To encourage her, they sent along letters and photographs and other mementos of their daughter. Barbara Klinner and the Birschbachs formed a friendship.

So I wrote another story about Barb Klinner's upcoming run for cancer. Barb thanked me for my interest and I dutifully sent in my donation. And so it goes in the column-writing business. I went on to the next thing, next column, and filed away Barb Klinner's mission in the recesses of my memory.

That is, until I went to the mailbox one day and found a big, thick envelope postmarked Wausau. It was from Barb Klinner. "What a difference we made," she wrote. She had run the race in San Diego and raised more than twice as much as she had pledged. In all, the six thousand runners in the Leukemia Society marathon raised over $15 million for cancer research, setting a record for the largest sporting-event fundraiser in history.

Beneath her letter to me was a stack of other letters from people who had read the column and wanted to contribute. They came from people like Mrs. Richard Mayton, whose husband died of leukemia at age ninety-five; Leland and Cathryn Long of Hudson, who just wished her good luck; and Jeanne and Don Ruehlow of Prairie du Chen, whose son Danny was diagnosed with a rare form of leukemia a few years ago but "is doing just great." She was overwhelmed by the response.

"It was incredible," Barb told me. "You realize just how many people out there really care. It's just so humbling."

Like any competitive person, Barb is never happy with her performance. She wanted to finish the 26.2 miles in under four hours but didn't meet her mark. It was terribly hot and humid and there wasn't enough water to go around and there were thousands of racers confined to a two-lane road.

"My feet are more sore from being stepped on than from running," she said. To add insult to injury, the plane she boarded for the trip home was rammed by a baggage cart and delayed. By the time she landed at the Appleton airport, it was midnight and she still had a two-hour drive ahead.

"And then we walked into the terminal, and there were Sue Birschbach's parents," she said. "They found out what flight we were on, drove two hours from Mequon to meet our plane, and they were carrying a big banner that said Congratulations, Barb!!"

It was, to understate things, the most emotional—and thoroughly gratifying—moment that occurred anywhere in the world on that particular day.

"I thought about Sue Birschbach and her courage all through that race," said Barb Klinner. "The whole sequence of events changed my life. We accomplished something really worthwhile. I'm more optimistic than ever that a cure for cancer will be found. And all those wonderful people who wrote all those letters and sent donations, I can't find the words to thank them."

She stopped talking for a moment to catch her breath.

"And getting to know the Birschbachs has been wonderful," she added. "I think we are going to be friends for a long, long time."

Barb and her husband kept in touch with the Birschbachs for years. They visited them at their home in Mequon—even going to the giant Birschbach family reunion—and Sue Birschbach's parents in turn visited them in

Wausau. Over time they haven't remained as close, but, as Barb hastens to say, it's only because they both have huge clans—Barb is one of ten children and the Birschbachs had ten of their own—and the family demands are formidable.

Barb has not slowed. She has run lots of marathons over the years to raise money, and she was chairman of the local chapter of the Susan G. Komen Foundation, raising $250,000 in the inaugural run for breast cancer research. Then, she said, she quit running marathons—and switched to hundred-mile ultramarathons.

Not long ago, she ran what she called a "solo ultramarathon-plus"—120 miles—to raise money for a pediatric oncology waiting room at the Marshfield Clinic. She ran in memory of Treyden Kurtzweil, a one-year-old boy who died of cancer. His parents wanted to create a warm, comfortable space at the clinic for families with children suffering from cancer. Sue started running to raise money for "Treyden's Cabin" at 5 a.m. one morning and ran until 5 p.m. the following day.

"I decided to run ten miles for every month that Treyden lived," she said.

Barb and Mark Klinner have also found time to raise four children, including two they adopted from Ethiopia seven years ago. In the middle of all this living, ironically and sadly, Barb's younger brother Don Brushaber was diagnosed with leukemia and died. Despite all her experience in oncology, and all the comfort and support she has given to cancer-stricken families in her lifetime, she said that when cancer strikes a member of your own family, all your professional experience goes out the window.

"It's entirely different," she said. "You are just like everyone else."

She said that reading the story about Sue Birschbach twenty years ago and then making the decision to act—"personally, not just professionally"—had been a springboard in her life. "I think it provided some comfort to the Birschbach family," she said. "That's all I ever wanted to do, just give them comfort."

# YOU CAN'T TATTOO A SOAP BUBBLE

## Evelyn Ann Fefer

Evelyn Fefer was our son Brendan's first-grade teacher at Richards School in Whitefish Bay. She was short in stature but long on dedication and discipline. By the time my son invaded her classroom, she had been teaching first grade since Harry Truman was president. She was old-school and no nonsense.

Unfortunately, our boy Brendan had his own way and it did not mirror Miss Fefer's. It had been a glacial year for both of them when, sometime in late spring, Miss Fefer invited my wife and me in for a little chat. The gist of her message, delivered delicately but with no room for misunderstanding, was that our six-year-old boy would benefit from a repeat of first grade.

We were devastated, affronted, angered. No parent wants to hear that. But eventually we saw the wisdom of Miss Fefer's ways and agreed to heed her advice. Days later: "You need to tell him that he's going to do first grade over again," my wife said.

"I need to tell him? You're his mother. You're the tactful one. You tell him."

"No," she insists, "you're much better at this sort of thing. After all, you're a newspaper editor. You make a living delivering bad news."

I was not going to win this argument. I waited until the last day of Brendan's first pass at first grade. I had never seen one little man in short pants and a Masters of the Universe T-shirt look so incredibly liberated. It was as if he had just walked out of a year in solitary confinement, squinting into the morning sun.

"Let's go to the movies," I suggest. I don't say anything about an end-of-the-school-year celebration. We pass a park bench perched on a bluff at Atwater Park overlooking Lake Michigan. I park the car. We walk to the bench and take a couple of seats.

We are gazing out at the blue-gray water of the big lake. "You know, Bren," I begin, "a guy doesn't always get things right the first time. Sometimes I do something at work and then my boss tells me that I can do better. So I do it over. You get my drift?"

"Right, Daddy," the boy says. I am not sure he understands me. He is watching sailboats at sea, swinging his little legs in those little blue sneakers, back and forth, to and fro. This is a boy without a care in the world. I don't feel good about this.

"Well, that's the way it went with you and first grade. You didn't get it right the first time. Know what I mean?" Brendan stops rocking, then swivels toward me, a mix of fear—and yes, loathing—in his eyes.

"Well, I'm not doing first grade again," he says. "I know that."

"No, I think you are," I say.

"No, I think I am not," the kid snaps back. "Maybe you forgot, Daddy, but I already graduated first grade."

"Yes, but you need a do-over," I say. "And this time you'll have a different teacher than Miss Fefer."

"I don't care who it is, I am not doing first grade again," he vows. I know that now is the time for deeper explanation. Now is the time to put this thing in perspective for the little man. I choose a less reflective approach.

"Yes, you are," I announce. "This discussion is officially over. Now we are going to the movies and we are going to have a really good time." And with that, we get up and leave.

Many years later, after the guy in the Masters of the Universe shirt had graduated from Marquette University High School and was on his way to college, I wrote about Evelyn Ann Fefer.

Everything the indomitable Evelyn Ann Fefer ever needed to know—or for that matter, everything you and I ever needed to know—was learned teaching first and second grades for over forty years. All of life's essential lessons played out in a classroom full of little girls and boys rarely taller than a yardstick.

One of her first graders was our boy, Brendan. For an entire school year we were subjected to a barrage of what came to be known as Fefer-isms, a never-ending supply of smart sayings pulled from her bottomless "learning sack." Over the years, I came to appreciate the wisdom of Miss Fefer, as the pint-sized lady was respectfully referred to. During the year my son had her as his teacher, however, there were moments when I had enough.

For example, if Brendan and I were having an argument and I announced that I had heard just about enough, he would reply, "Miss Fefer says to keep the vents on the side of your head open. They are tools for learning."

If he got in trouble for going his own way at school—a euphemism if ever there was one—and I told him that he had to learn how to behave in a group, he would counter, "But Miss Fefer says to be a somebody, not an everybody."

Or if I was angry and about to blow my top, he would take a step back, look me in the eye from three feet below, and say, confidently, "Miss Fefer says not to lose your temper because nobody wants to find it. Miss Fefer says that anger is only one letter away from danger. And Miss Fefer says that if you point a finger at someone, just remember that you are pointing three at yourself!" At which point the boy, sensing that he had crossed the rhetorical line, would usually run.

We threw a party to celebrate Brendan's high school graduation. We invited our friends and he invited his. High on his list, alongside a bunch of seventeen-year-old boys with dreadlocks and buzz cuts, earrings, and tattoos that announced undying devotion to a rock band called Phish, was the great one's name: Miss Fefer.

We hadn't seen her in a few years, though she checked in regularly by telephone. She hadn't changed a bit. She was charming and animated and full of good humor. More than seventy years out, she was the undisputed hit of the party. Everybody who had kids or grandkids or had ever been a kid was magnetically drawn to Evelyn Ann Fefer. And although she retired a few years ago, her legendary "learning sack" still overflowed with wisdom.

"The most important thing I learned in all those years was that a child has to feel that somebody really cares," she said. "That's what I tried to make each child realize: you are somebody special."

She saw a lot of changes in those years, not all of them for the better. Too many families coming apart, too many professional pressures on young parents, too many divorces, far too many fads in child-rearing. And more than a few too many self-absorbed parents who forgot it was the children they brought into the world who were most important.

"I remember a little boy whose parents had joint custody," she said. "He would spend the week with his mother and weekends with his father. Every Friday he would arrive at school with a little suitcase in his hand. I always met him at the door and put that suitcase in my own closet so other children wouldn't ask him about it. I wanted him to feel secure.

"One day his father came to pick him up and this man was very proud of himself for showing up. He wanted me to praise him! I said, 'Praise you? It's your son who needs and deserves praise. You owe it to him. You're his father!'"

She also was frequently distressed by the growing number of children on medication.

"Don't get me started," said Miss Fefer, only she was already launched. "It got to the point where they wanted to prescribe a drug for every child that wiggled. I was opposed to it. One time at a meeting I stood up and said so. I said those drugs affect a child's appetite and therefore his growth and nutrition. Who wouldn't have trouble paying attention?

"This little chickie stood up and said, 'Evy, you've just been teaching too long. You can't stand change.' I said, 'I've been fortunate to teach a long, long time, little lady, long enough to know that a child who is sedated cannot learn.'"

She was quiet for a moment.

"The term 'attention deficit disorder' is a fancy term for kids," she said.

A few days after the graduation party, the phone rang. It was Miss Fefer. She was just calling to say that she had a wonderful time, that she was immensely proud of "my boy Brendan," and that she just knew he would have great fun in college and beyond. "Because Brendan knows that only in the dictionary does 'success' come before 'work,'" she said, a Feferism ever at the ready.

I thanked her for coming. I told her how much it meant to Brendan to have his favorite teacher and perpetual guiding light on hand. And I told her how much she had meant to all of us through the years.

"No, no, no, Steve," she corrected me. "It was you who gave me the greatest gift, the privilege of teaching your child. And you know, the greatest gifts always come unwrapped."

One day, after she had been retired for a few years, I received a letter from Evy Fefer. I was on to a new business undertaking and she wanted to wish me well. She inquired after Brendan—he was halfway through college then—and the rest of the family. She said that "light travels faster than sound but I work in reverse: I sound off and hope the light will bring a little laughter." And then she went on for pages with Feferism after Feferism: You can't sew a button on a lemon meringue pie. You can't turn a mushroom into a rose. You can't tattoo a soap bubble. I can teach you how to open an umbrella, but I can't make it stop raining.

Miss Fefer died on June 16, 2010. She was eighty-eight.

Although I knew her for years, I didn't know much about her private life, other than that she lived with her sister, Charlotte, in an apartment in Shorewood. In one account I read after her death, someone reported that she was born in Russia—another account said Poland—and had been forbidden to attend the local school because she was Jewish. Supposedly she had been taught in a makeshift classroom in the loft of a barn, turned into a school for children who were not welcome. I tried to get to the bottom of her story but didn't make much progress. So I don't know how much of this and that is true but I suspect it is the rough outline of her life. And if so, it explains—at least in part—her relentless dedication to teaching and her predisposition to protect small children.

# THE ROAD TO REDEMPTION

## Ed Thompson

I got to know Governor Tommy Thompson just a little. I first met him when he was minority leader in the state legislature and was not too affectionately known as Dr. No. Years later, he invited me to breakfast at the Governor's Mansion in Maple Bluff when I was managing editor of the *Milwaukee Journal*. We had pancakes and sausage and, if I recall correctly, a polite disagreement or two about the way the paper was covering his administration. And one memorable night at the White House Correspondents' Dinner in Washington, I introduced him to Barbra Streisand. (That's a story for another time and place.) Overall, I thought he was eminently pragmatic and a good governor. But with all due respect, if I had to drive cross-country with one of the Thompson boys, I would have picked the

"I learned to conquer my fear of failure," said Eddie Thompson. "I learned that there is great strength in kindness and love is the only reality." Photo courtesy of the *Tomah Journal*.

"younger, smarter brother," as Eddie Thompson described himself. Where Tommy was cool and calculating—after all, he was a very successful politician who went on to serve as a cabinet secretary in President George W. Bush's administration—Eddie was warm, welcoming, wide open for business, and utterly-but-charmingly unfiltered.

When he was in the eighth grade growing up in Elroy, Ed Thompson heard there was a kid who lived over in Mauston who thought he could lick him. Ed found this hard to fathom. So one day he left home and walked eleven miles to Mauston to see for himself.

"His name was Nug and I invited him to fight," Ed remembers. Not long afterward, Nug showed up at the Elroy fair with his older brother.

"We went out behind the swimming pool," says Ed. "It was a two-hit fight. I hit him and he hit the ground."

Eddie Thompson enjoyed a good fistfight. When he finished high school, he couldn't wait to get to the University of Wisconsin and join the boxing team. Unfortunately, the year before he arrived, a college fighter named Charlie Mohr died in the ring, and the sport was dropped. So Ed spent mornings in Madison sparring with a law student, working hard to refine his skills. Later he fought in the Navy, Golden Gloves, and in amateur bouts around the state.

"In the eighties I competed in those Tough Man tournaments like you see on TV," he says, smiling at the memory of it. "I was in a tournament in La Crosse and I was the oldest guy fighting. I never lost, but finally the doc wouldn't let me back in the ring. I guess I was pretty well beat up. I finished fourth but I won all my fights."

He had a boxing style similar to a guy named Rocky Marciano. "I took five punches to land one," Ed says with undisguised pride. "I got used to getting punched pretty good. But if I could land one, I could usually put 'em down."

Allan Edward Thompson, fifty-five, is, in his own words, the "younger, smarter" brother of Tommy Thompson. Like the governor, he won a political match last week, the fight to become mayor of Tomah, a little city in west central Wisconsin. He got in the race in the first place because he was angry about a police raid on his bar, Mr. Ed's Tee Pee Supper Club. He was busted for allowing video poker.

Anyway, that was then and this is now, the first day of the rest of his life as a politician. We are sitting in a back booth at the Tee Pee the day after his election. The soon-to-be mayor bears a striking resemblance to his famous older brother—wavy haired, ruddy faced, raw boned, formidable. He's five feet eight inches tall and weighs in at 220 pounds, and when he shakes your hand you would swear it was stuck between a bus and a brick wall.

I had decided awhile back that I wanted to meet Eddie Thompson. He had the perfect pedigree. He did time as a boxer, bar owner, cook at a federal prison, professional poker player, and county snow-plower. He was also the governor's very outspoken and controversial younger brother. Every time I came across him in the news, he was in some sort of scrape, trading punches with the cops or the district attorney or—in a little incident that could have been a lot worse—getting stabbed in the gut during a brouhaha with two butchers.

"The guy who stabbed me came to my victory party last night," Ed says, dismissing the incident. "He's a good fellow and a good friend."

Most of what I read about Ed Thompson was not flattering. Ed was the black sheep, the politically incorrect brother who, on occasion, must have made his brother the governor wish he were an only child.

But I didn't find Ed Thompson to be anything like the character portrayed in his press clippings. The guy who walked to Mauston to slug Nug is an interesting, intelligent, introspective, articulate, philosophical, thoughtful man. Forget Roger Clinton and Billy Carter and all the other cartoon-character political brothers he's been compared to. Maybe I'm not the most discerning guy in the state, but Ed struck me as more of a cross between Jesse Ventura and Mohandas K. Gandhi.

"Tommy called me last night after we won," he says. "He said, 'Watch your mouth. That's the first thing. The second is to keep your friends close and your enemies closer.'"

I said I thought that was sound political advice from a big brother who ought to know.

"Most of it," agrees Ed, shrugging it off, "except that I don't really believe in enemies."

To understand that statement you need to know just how far Ed has traveled in his life. By his own account, he was married to a wonderful woman for eighteen years and had four terrific kids. The marriage, he says, ended in divorce because he "screwed it up." After that he sold the Tee Pee to a guy who lasted all of one month in the business. And then he leased it to another guy and things went from bad to worse.

"My life was a mess," Ed confesses. "I was totally broke. I was forty-nine years old, living alone in a house with a German shepherd named Ace. The only income I had was $250 a month from a trailer I was renting. I was down-and-out and facing the one thing I feared most of all in life: failure.

"I was spending a lot of time walking the [Elroy-Sparta bike] trail, walking and talking with Ace, just thinking. I was living off my neighbor's leftovers. I sold my old Cadillac convertible to get heat in the house.

You know those dog biscuits called Bonz? Those are great dunkers. I shared them with Ace. It's true and I'm not ashamed to tell you. Trust me: when you're broke, you're broke."

During that dark night of the soul, the toughest kid in Elroy, the guy who never minded taking five punches to land one, says he started reading everything he could lay his hands on—books on philosophy, religion, morality, mysticism, Confucianism, and the Holy Bible.

"I learned a lot of things that year," says the mayor-elect. "I learned that if you let fear into your heart, it will dominate your life. I had always been a fighter and a get-even kind of guy. I was mad because I had a good business and turned it over to someone else and they let me down. I had a lot of hate in my heart. But it took me that year to learn that hatred is a load that's much too heavy to carry in life."

Ed Thompson hit rock bottom one Thanksgiving Day. He and Ace sat together eating a leftover hamburger hot dish from one of the neighbors. He remembers saying to himself, "If I ever get out of this hole I've dug, I'll never eat alone again"—no offense to Ace.

At the time, Ed owed $78,000 to a variety of creditors. A guy named Duane Weed from the Bank of Necedah decided to take a chance: he loaned Ed Thompson $80,000. Ed paid his debts, and with $2,000 sitting in his pocket and resolve in his heart, he began the long climb out of the depths of despair.

The Tee Pee had been shuttered for four months. Ed started putting it back in order, cleaning and repairing it so he could reopen the bar and make a living. He slept on the floor of the supper club because he didn't have enough money for gas to drive six miles home to his trailer. First the bar reopened, then the restaurant. Slowly but surely, business picked up.

Today, Mr. Ed's Tee Pee serves about four hundred people at its Friday fish fry. On Saturday night the place is packed to the rafters. Ed Thompson also owns five buildings along the city block where his supper club sits on Superior Street. "Business," he says, slowly savoring every syllable, "is real good."

Last Thursday he got engaged to his girlfriend of six years, Tina Turner. And on April 18, this guy who not long ago was dunking dog biscuits in a coffee cup and sharing a handout Thanksgiving dinner with a dog named Ace will be officially sworn in as mayor. He is philosophical about his life.

"I have learned to live in the moment with the best that I have," Ed Thompson says. "I learned to conquer my fear of failure. I learned that no one gains if someone loses. I learned that there is great strength in kindness and love is the only reality."

A blonde named Doris Harris stops by our booth and interrupts Mayor Ed with a kiss on the cheek. "I am so goddamn happy, Eddie," she says, "I hardly know what to say."

"You've said enough," says Ed, "and you've done enough. Let me buy you one."

"Like I said, my life is an adventure," says Ed, turning back to our conversation. "When I think back to those dark days, I can hardly believe how far I've come. I enjoy every minute of my life. And I can't wait to walk across the street to city hall and open door number two."

Eddie Thompson died in October 2011 after losing a fight—and this is a guy who didn't lose many fights—with pancreatic cancer. He was mayor of Tomah for two terms—2002-4 and 2008-10. He also ran for governor as a Libertarian in 2002. The chief criticism leveled against him when he ran for governor—a job his brother held from 1987 to 2001—was that he lacked experience in Madison. "We are the third most heavily taxed state in the union," he told me when I stopped to see him at the Tee Pee. "If that's what you get when you have experienced people who know what they're doing, I say 'Praise the Lord' that I don't!" He didn't win that election, but he captured the largest percentage of the vote for a third-party candidate in sixty years. He also did one other thing before he died: every year he hosted a free Thanksgiving dinner at the Tee Pee for anyone who needed a meal and some company.

# A MILLION MILES TO GO

## Don and Cathryn Tredinnick

I have always been—as my mother charitably described me—a "busy boy."
I was like that from the moment I popped out of the womb. I was in a state
of perpetual motion. Over time I came to equate my movement with a
sense of accomplishment. Moving was living; dawdling was dying.

Movers were clearly life's winners. What were they winning? I haven't a
clue. I was too busy running to give it much thought.

There was actually a period in my life—from about 1994 until the turn
of the century—when I very deliberately decided that sleeping was an utter
waste of time. So during that phase I went to bed at 1:30 a.m. and got up at
5:30. It took me six years to figure out that getting about half the requisite

"Have you ever heard the expression that the joy is in the journey, not the destination?" asked Cathryn Tredinnick. "Well, it wouldn't hurt you to consider it." Photos courtesy of Cathryn Tredinnick.

dose of rest each night was not making me twice as productive but, rather, twice as muddle-headed.

One day during what I refer to as the frantic years, my friend Bill Beach—a man who knew how to rest—approached me with an idea for a column: His friend Ed Lindner, a veterinarian in Dodgeville, knew a couple who retired a few years back and decided to travel every federal, state, county, and local road in Wisconsin. Bill wasn't sure how long they had been at it or how many miles they had covered, but he thought it was just the kind of odd notion that was perfect for my "State of Mind." I thought so too. People in a permanent state of motion. People, I thought, just . . . like . . . me! So I went—really fast—to meet these kindred souls.

We all know people who retire, turn the key, and head for exotic destinations that they had neither the time nor money to visit while working. They cruise the Caribbean, island hop in Hawai'i, or maybe even climb Mount Kilimanjaro (I knew a woman who turned sixty and did just that).

Not so Don and Cathryn Tredinnick of Dodgeville. They, too, wanted to see the wonders of the world in retirement, but as it turns out, they didn't want to stray too terribly far from home. But their dream was nonetheless ambitious: travel all the US, state, county, and town roads in Wisconsin—approximately 1.1 million miles in all.

"We've been at it for six years now," deadpans Don, sixty-nine, an accountant by trade.

And how much have you covered?

"We're about seven-eighths done with Iowa County," he says.

I am shocked. I am also a little annoyed. I have made this trip to Tredinnickville under false pretenses. These people haven't even covered one whole county. Do they know they're—not to put too harsh a point on it—losing the race?

I go ahead and tell them that, while I hate to be the bearer of bad news, there are seventy-two counties in Wisconsin—over a million miles to cover—and they are galactically failing. They are never going to reach their goal, not even come close. I expect them to counter with something, anything. I would.

"No, I don't suppose we are," says Don, agreeing with me. He laughs. "Not much chance of that."

I soon learn that the Tredinnicks are not exactly bounding out of bed 365 days a year, diving into the family sedan, and manically driving hither and yon to achieve their goal. Quite the contrary. They have pretty much concluded—no, willingly accepted—that their goal is unattainable. So they have decided to take their own sweet time.

"I mean, just doing the county roads in Wisconsin would probably take a person a hundred years," says Don. "I'm not sure I'm going to be around that long."

Their plan of attack is glacial. Generally they confine their touring to Sunday afternoons, starting at four o'clock. They drive fifty or sixty miles, always observe the speed limit, always get home before dark, and don't venture out when the roads or weather or both are lousy. They revel in the scenery and keep track of it all on a dog-eared map they keep in the family "safe."

If this doesn't sound like anyone's idea of wanderlust, well, tough toenails. It's the Tredinnicks' and they love it. "There's no end to the beauty of Iowa County," says Cathryn, sixty-four, who along with her husband was born and raised in this general neighborhood. "I love the country roads, rolling hills, wildlife, and change of seasons. It's always fascinating and it never gets old."

"I love to be driving along and see an old, abandoned farmstead," Don chimes in. "You'll see an old farmhouse that hasn't been lived in for fifty years, a yard with overgrown grass and junk, and an empty barn. I like to imagine what might have gone on in that empty place when it was alive, someone's home, a family's livelihood, and center of their world. I let my imagination run wild. Frankly, it makes me pretty emotional."

The Tredinnicks talk about their travels in Iowa County, Wisconsin, like someone else might talk about a trip to Tahiti or Kathmandu. They discuss the mysteries of Lovers Lane north of Rewey to Dry Dog Road off County Q to Norwegian Hollow just outside of Dodgeville. The words they use resemble the language of passionate travelers describing whole countries, even continents. They don't simply say they took a casual ride to Mineral Point or Cobb; they reference trips to the "west" or "northeast" in a way that—if you didn't know better—makes you think they've just blown in from a mule trek into the Grand Canyon or a hike along the rocky coast of Maine.

In truth, they've been no farther than little farm towns like Wald-wick or Edmund or Clyde, places you can hardly find on a map. And while they talk movingly about the scenery they've taken in along the way, turns out it's not the actual traveling that drives them. "We just like the time together," says Cathryn. "That's really what matters to us."

"It's the time when we talk about our lives, our children, our what-would-happen-ifs, our plans and dreams," says Don. "The times when we talk about the things that are just between the two of us."

The Tredinnicks have been married for almost half a century. They tell me that they have never had what would count as a certifiable argument in that time. They blow off steam in one another's direction from time to time, but neither can remember anything that would qualify as a serious disagreement. Their time traversing the back roads of Wisconsin—let's be honest, we're talking about the back roads of Iowa County—is almost always a sweet and relaxing time.

Well, almost.

"The one thing that Don does that gets me worried is when he just up and pulls off the side of the road to highlight the map with his marker," says Cathryn. "He insists on doing this right after we have finished a particular road. And sometimes he doesn't bother to put on the directional signal. I fear that one of these days we are going to get rear-ended."

That's the closest they come to conflict. It's incredible to me, having grown up in a family—immediate and extended—where conflict was as predictable as the change of seasons. If we weren't clashing, we weren't living. These Tredinnick people, by contrast, are peaceful, polite, soft-spoken, civilized. I should have noticed right away. They love each other. I am in the presence of love.

I don't dare say it, of course, but if quibbling over when to highlight the map qualifies as the most stress-filled moment in your forty-six-year marriage, you are still honeymooning. But I do ask Don why he just doesn't wait until he gets home to highlight the map. "Because I might forget where we've been," he says. Makes sense to me.

The simple sounds and sights are always the most pleasurable. On a recent Sunday evening, they drove from Dodgeville to Spring Green on Highway 23, which is Frank Lloyd Wright country. The sunset was glorious and the whitetail deer were just sitting down to supper in the cornfields.

"I counted between thirty and forty," says Cathryn, breathlessly, "and I'm sure I didn't count them all. It was thrilling."

On another recent Sunday afternoon, they went west to a place near the tiny village of Linden, to his grandparents' farm where Don was raised. It was abandoned fifty years ago. Patchy grass and stringy weeds obscured what had once been a happy place that produced bushels of cherished memories for a boy.

"I left that farm back in 1943," Don says. "Now it is empty and lonely compared to the way it used to be. To me, it represents history, my family's history. I walked inside and I cried for the pure emptiness of lives long ago."

But tell me truthfully, isn't there something about actually driving 1.1 million miles and covering all those Wisconsin roads and seeing the beauty that exists beyond one single county in the southwest corner of the state—to see the great forests up north where the loggers worked, and the majesty and pristine beauty of Lake Superior, and Door County along Green Bay or fishing villages along Lake Michigan? Doesn't that possibility tug at you just a little bit?

"Not really," says Cathryn.

"Not much," says Don.

"Have you ever heard the expression that the joy is in the journey, not the destination?" Cathryn asks me. I can tell she feels a little sorry for my restless self. I've heard it, I say, but I never really thought much about it.

"Well, it wouldn't hurt you to consider it," says Cathryn.

A journey of 1.1 million miles, to butcher a proverb from the Chinese philosopher Lao Tzu, begins with a single tank of regular gas. As far as the Tredinnicks are concerned, the rest of the world will just have to wait. I wonder aloud if they ever dwell on things and places they may never see?

"Not really," says Don.

"To tell you the truth," says Cathryn, "I'm not all that eager to finish Iowa County. I'm afraid it will end too soon."

Don Tredinnick, an eminently practical man with a dry sense of humor, died in December 2000, just a few months after celebrating his fiftieth wedding anniversary. Cathryn turned eighty-seven in 2018, and while she misses her husband each and every day, she doesn't let much grass grow under her feet. She is caught up in the lives of her seven children—six boys and a girl—as well as thirteen grandchildren and nine great-grandchildren. They are scattered from Wisconsin to Minnesota to Colorado to Texas. She has a full life, and based upon my thirty-minute catch-up conversation with her the other day, she has lost none of her appetite for life or laughter.

Of course, I have to ask: "Did you ever finish traveling all the roads in Iowa County?"

"Yes, we did," Cathryn says. "We surely did."

And the rest of Wisconsin? "No," she says. "We were never going to do that. Nowadays, though, I drive as far as La Crosse to see one of our boys and his family. And from there we drive up north to the cabin in Hayward. That's enough."

Cathryn spends a lot of her time in the neighborhood with "the girls," a gang of widows who get together and make mischief weekly. She volunteers at the Dodgeville hospital, is a member of the local Women's Club, and stays active with her church. She and Don made regular trips to Ho-Chunk Casino in Wisconsin Dells, but she gave that up when he died. Like everything else, at the casino they had a very deliberate plan of attack.

"I had a pint jar and I'd save my quarters," she explains. "When we had forty quarters, we'd go to Ho-Chunk and play the slots. I'd play until I was out of quarters but Don—you remember that Don was an accountant, right?—he would stop as soon as he got ahead. I think it's fair to say they didn't get rich off us."

What, I ask her years later, was the secret to what struck me as a wonderful marriage? "Well, Don always said that he made the money and I raised the kids. I cooked him three meals a day for fifty years. We were practical people. We both grew up on farms. It was good." She paused in thought for a long moment. "I guess mainly we enjoyed each other's company. We never got carried away. We had good friends, but we liked each other's company more than anything else."

I remember the Tredinnicks well. Never forgot them. They embodied the best of Wisconsin: they were kind, considerate, and naturally modest—the Badger trifecta. And, lest I forget, naturally practical.

"Don is buried in the Eastside Cemetery," says Cathryn. "I stop by and say hi, then I go just past the cemetery where the city lets you dump your yard waste. It's really convenient."

I tease her a little. "I'm sure Don would appreciate your efficiency," I say. "Not only do you stop and see him, but you get rid of your grass clippings too."

The lady, who knows every mile of Iowa County, laughs. "I think he would," she says. "In fact I know he would."

# POSTSCRIPT

We had a singularly inspiring English professor when I was an undergraduate at Colgate University. His name was Jonathan Kistler. He
taught a popular course on Shakespeare. I approached him for advice
in my junior year after I landed a microscopic role in the university
theater's production of *Hamlet*. For a week or so, I contemplated a career on the stage. He was generous and encouraging, even though I
was pretty sure he thought I was better suited for a career in plumbing
supplies. The experience ended up crushing my theatrical ambitions
flat but it did have a couple of unforeseen benefits: I can still recite most
of Polonius's advice to Laertes ("Neither a borrower nor a lender be,"
which I've used with limited success in counseling my children) as well
as Hamlet's sad soliloquy ("I have of late—but wherefore I know not—
lost all my mirth"), which once got me a date with a really charming
lady from Virginia who was mad for Shakespeare and momentarily
mistook me for Laurence Olivier. It could have been the beer.

Anyway, Professor Kistler had a rare gift that, in my experience, only a precious few teachers possessed—he made his subjects come absolutely alive in the classroom!

Two years after I graduated, Jonathan Kistler was invited to give the commencement address at Colgate. He told the seniors that, while he had personally attended something like forty-five commencement speeches through the years, he could only remember one—a three-paragraph summary that he had come across in the *New York Times*. It made a simple point: Great success was sure to come, the speaker had assured his young audience, but it was probably more important to deal with the inevitability of failure.

Kistler recommended three books for the graduates to read: *The Education of Henry Adams* by Henry Adams, Reinhold Niebuhr's *The Children of Light and the Children of Darkness*, and *Crime and Punishment* by Fyodor Dostoyevsky. The professor extracted important life lessons from each of these great books—lessons about how you might as well accept that human life is basically unpredictable and frequently unintelligible; that no man can "claim a genuine optimism unless he has first come to grips with this thing called pessimism"; and that—my personal favorite—*in learning to accept people the way they are (as ordinary human beings) we learn to accept our ordinary selves.*

But he liked Dostoyevsky's take on living best: "It can make us see the extraordinary quality of what we usually think of as the ordinariness of life, the life we are living day-to-day: eating and drinking and talking . . . and the shopping and the tuition payments and the children. And all of our successes, which you know are good things to have, and all of our failures, which are inevitable."

Jonathan Kistler concluded his send-off better than anyone ever ended a commencement address before or since: "The novel can best immortalize the ordinary life, the kind of life your parents have led, and the kind of life you, too, will no doubt lead eventually. It is the kind of life that perhaps in the end breaks your heart, but it will fill your heart before it breaks it."

My mother would say it's a good trade-off.

# Acknowledgments

I'm sure there are authors who can write a book without help from another living soul. I am not one of those people. I needed the occasional pat on the head or persistent kick in the pants to compose this little love letter to Wisconsin. So, I would like to recognize the people who inspired, counseled, encouraged, occasionally shamed and sometimes just told me to stop whining and get back to writing. My eternal gratitude goes out to:

Ms. Pixie Louise Krintzman, who frequently pulled me out of the mud when I got stuck; Josh Modell, for his patience, kindness, and good humor, but most of all for his exceptional editorial skills; Brady Williamson, my longtime legal counselor, spiritual advisor, and friend, who contributed, among other things, invaluable insight into the Wisconsin character; my late friends Bill and Natalie Beach, who, directly or indirectly, steered me toward so many of the people who populate this book; Bob Smith, who was always there to help no matter what was needed; Dan Cattau, a literate man and accomplished editor, who helped as much as he could, given what he had to work with—me; Herm Tschudy, a first-rate friend, who, through countless conversations while hiking the wilds of Badger Ordnance, always listened, frequently laughed, and told

me that things were going to turn out just fine; Dr. Paul D. Martin—
The Doc—who was a willing accomplice on so many of my adventures;
David K. Schafer, for his great friendship and unwavering opinion that
I could write a book that somebody, somewhere might pay for; Susan
Bing Hannah, who got me to Wisconsin in the first place; Sig Gissler,
who told me never to forget that "Wisconsin is not just a state; it's a state
of mind"; Jamie E. Hannah and James Moody, for their critical creative
direction; Brendan Bing Hannah, for letting me loot his life to manufac-
ture many, many columns, including one very special one that appears
in this book; Elizabeth Trieu, for convincing Brendan that "looting lives
is what writers do," and so, just live with it; Stephen N. Hunt, because
he has stuck by me through thick and thin for more than fifty years and
promised to buy several copies; Hal Bergan, a longtime friend and in-
satiable reader, who first suggested that my "State of Mind" columns
might be the basis for a book; and, I suppose, the honorable Michael G.
Laskis, attorney-at-law, who, once, after I confessed to having a pretty
unproductive day of book writing, commented, "It must be difficult to
make a good story out of a life that really hasn't been all that interesting,"
then had the audacity to ask that his name be included in the dedication
but, failing that, allowed as how he would settle for a small acknowledg-
ment. So this is it, Mick.

And, in one fell swoop, I'd like to acknowledge all the Wisconsin people
profiled in these pages.

Plus, in no particular order: George Stanley of the *Milwaukee Journal
Sentinel*; Andy Thompson of the Appleton *Post Crescent*; Dan Reiland of
the *Eau Claire Leader-Telegram*; Tom Enwright, formerly of the *Wisconsin
Rapids Daily Tribune*; Dennis Wiemer; Larry and Mike Tronrud; Barbara
Schultz Gomes; Cindy Kort and Jayme Bleick-Baehnman; Brian
Hulsether; Allison Beach Hellman; Nancy Larson-Manthe; Kay Bauer;
Jack Berndt and the Sauk Prairie Area Historical Society; Kathleen
McGwin, the sage of Marquette County; Ben Strand, who loves Wiscon-
sin and knows where its history is hiding; Marna Boyle; the late Donald
"Jake" Gattshall, who reminded me regularly that we lived in "a little

piece of paradise"; Jonathan Eig; Scott Simon; Dr. Bernard Easterday; Peter Lichtner; and Andrea Waala of the Museum of Wisconsin Art.

Meanwhile, I want to offer my eternal gratitude to the very professional team at the University of Wisconsin Press—particularly Raphael Kadushin, Gwen Walker, Sheila McMahon, and the ever-persistent Anna Muenchrath—who encouraged, counseled, and instructed me every step of the way. (They also helped me march a pretty straight line because, alas, I am a guy given to wandering.)

And heartfelt thanks to all those other folks who contributed to this book but whose names escape me at the moment. You get older, you forget some things.

**STEVE HANNAH** spent almost two decades as a pretty good reporter, sometime columnist, and managing editor of the *Milwaukee Journal*. He then devoted twelve years of his life to writing a syndicated column called "State of Mind." The last ten years of his career were spent as CEO of *The Onion*, America's Finest News Source.

He once spent a winter night in northern Wisconsin with a guy who invented a contraption that would take the whole shell off a hard-boiled egg by employing an electrifying two-handed thrust that resembled the Heimlich maneuver. While the experience didn't exactly change his life, it was a lot more interesting than covering the state legislature.

He divides his time these days between his home on the Wisconsin River in Sauk County and Austin, Texas.